Exploring White Fragility

Exploring White Fragility

Debating the Effects of Whiteness Studies on America's Schools

Christopher Paslay

ROWMAN & LITTLEFIELD
Lanham • Boulder • New York • London

Published by Rowman & Littlefield
An imprint of The Rowman & Littlefield Publishing Group, Inc.
4501 Forbes Boulevard, Suite 200, Lanham, Maryland 20706
www.rowman.com

6 Tinworth Street, London SE11 5AL, United Kingdom

Copyright © 2020 by The Rowman & Littlefield Publishing Group, Inc.

All rights reserved. No part of this book may be reproduced in any form or by any electronic or mechanical means, including information storage and retrieval systems, without written permission from the publisher, except by a reviewer who may quote passages in a review.

British Library Cataloguing in Publication Information Available

Library of Congress Cataloging-in-Publication Data Available

Library of Congress Control Number: 2020047775
IBSN 978-1-4758-5772-6 (cloth)
ISBN 978-1-4758-5773-3 (pbk.)
ISBN 978-1-4758-5774-0 (electronic)

For the hardworking teachers, students,
and parents of the School District of Philadelphia

Contents

Preface: Not All Whites Are Racially Illiterate	ix
Notes	xi
Acknowledgments	xiii
Introduction: The One-Sided Conversation	xv
Notes	xvii
1 The Tenets of Whiteness Studies	1
Multiculturalism vs. Antiracism	4
White Privilege and White Fragility	6
"Racism" and "White Supremacy"	9
Colorblindness and Individualism	12
Impact vs. Intent	15
Recommendations	18
Notes	19
2 Methodology	23
Overuse of Implicit Bias	24
The Dubious Nature of Microaggressions	28
Epistemological Problems	32
Recommendations	33
Notes	34
3 Anti-Bias Training	35
Mandatory vs. Voluntary Training	40
New York's Toxic Racial Environment	41
Recommendations	45
Notes	45
4 Culture Matters	47

	Asian Americans	49
	West Indian and African Immigrants	51
	The Racialization of Universal Values	54
	Recommendations	58
	Notes	58
5	Parents and Patriarchy	61
	Father Facts	62
	Parents and Educational Attainment	65
	Toxic Masculinity and Patriarchy	67
	Recommendations	69
	Notes	69
6	Assault on Learning	71
	Violence as a Coping Mechanism	73
	The Courage of Transparency	75
	Dedicated to Positive Change	78
	Recommendations	81
	Notes	82
7	Racial Disparities and School Discipline	85
	The School-to-Prison Pipeline	87
	Race-Based Discipline	89
	Discipline through the Eyes of Teachers	92
	Recommendations	94
	Notes	95
8	The Power of Expectations	97
	Stereotype Threat	102
	The American Dream	105
	Recommendations	110
	Notes	110
9	Solutions: Diversity Through Unity	113
	Leaving the Mind and Entering the Heart	117
	The Magic of Unity	120
	Recommendations	123
	Notes	124
Bibliography		125
Index		131
About the Author		139

Preface

Not All Whites Are Racially Illiterate

Robin DiAngelo, whose white fragility theory has become one of the most influential ideas about racism in America, believes the majority of whites in America are racially illiterate. In her book, *What Does It Mean To Be White?: Developing White Racial Literacy*, she describes how it's taken her years of intensive study and practice to be able to recognize how her life has been shaped by race, and goes on to list many of the advantages of being white, writing that although she is speaking for herself, "it is a rare white person who cannot recognize most of the privileges I identify."[1]

She begins with a section titled "Belonging," and explains how she was born into a culture where she was accepted racially, and how even *where* she was born and the conditions surrounding her birth were shaped by race—that the all-white hospital, in the all-white neighborhood, filled with the all-white mothers nursing their all-white babies, socialized her into believing whiteness was normal, free from "race," and that being white was associated with acceptance, privilege, and the luxury of not having to think about skin color.[2]

Curiously, my birth was the total opposite. My mother was nineteen when she had me, and my father was a twenty-one-year-old education student at Temple University. Recently married, they were renting a 900-square-foot rowhouse in Southwest Philadelphia, and had no health insurance. When my mother went into labor five days before Christmas in 1971, my father took her to what was then Misericordia Hospital at 54th and Cedar in the predominantly African American section of West Philadelphia, a health care facility that had a government-subsidized maternity clinic.

My mom knew immediately that they were in an all-black neighborhood as she saw the black Santa Clauses decorating the houses and lawns. As they drove through the streets my mom remembered feeling very aware of being white—as people on street corners and in SEPTA buses gave her extended glances and hard looks, wondering what her and my father were doing in their neighborhood.

She recalled the same experience as she sat in the waiting area of the hospital, as many of the patients were black. And when my mom gave birth to me and was recovering on the maternity ward and doting over me in the nursery, she remembered the stares of the black women, and recalled one of them commenting, "What is this skinny white girl doing here?" Granted, this was 1971, a much angrier time in America, where racial tension was overt and personal, not simply implicit or systemic.

To my parents' credit, they never became bitter or harbored any racial resentment. In fact, just the opposite: my father became a schoolteacher at John Bartram High School in the increasingly diverse neighborhood of Southwest Philadelphia, teaching business and coaching track and cross country. At this time we lived in Yeadon, Pennsylvania, a small suburb of Philadelphia. And when the neighborhood started to change demographically—when families from West Philly started to move into the area, my parents stayed put. When gang activity over a turf dispute started as a result, they stuck it out.

When fights and violence erupted, they tried to stay positive. It wasn't until I was assaulted outside the Yeadon movie theater that my parents considered moving. It was for safety reason, my dad insisted. When we finally did leave the neighborhood the summer before my freshman year in high school, I was beside myself. I was convinced my parents wanted to leave because all my friends were black, and because I'd completely fallen in love with this budding new cultural phenomenon called hip-hop—obsessing over rap music, breakdancing, graffiti art, and Run DMC.

Despite the move, I turned out okay. I became a Philadelphia public schoolteacher and track coach like my father. Students in my English classes have gone on to graduate college and become psychologists, teachers, business owners, and computer programmers. In 2015, a former pupil of mine graduated the United States Air Force Academy. On the track, my athletes have won Penn Relays medals, PIAA State Track and Field Championships, and have been awarded multiple academic and athletic scholarships.

In total, I've spent two decades working and interacting with teenagers and parents of all races and ethnic backgrounds in Philadelphia classrooms, on ballfields, and in the basements of churches. I'm also a certified secondary school counselor, with an MEd in Multicultural Education. I've read and studied Freire, Kozol, McIntosh, Feagin, Tatum, Banks, Helms, Frankenberg, Takaki, and multiple other scholars and researchers. And of course I've read and studied Robin DiAngelo, whose life and upbringing, though in some ways very similar, is worlds apart from mine.

I draw a parallel to DiAngelo's life not to deny whites have a systemic societal advantage over people of color—or to deny that my early life experiences were contextual, and that they took place in the microculture as opposed to the macroculture—but to show that DiAngelo's worldview is only a perspective of the whole, and should not be viewed as infallible or universally correct. I have a different insight into the dynamics of race and race relations, and these insights shouldn't be written off as "ignorant" or "illiterate."

Yet too often they are. I have attended scores of anti-bias workshops over the past twenty-three years—including one on white fragility headed by Robin DiAngelo—and have witnessed the usual patterns of Orwellian indoctrination emerge from facilitators and professors. They are always the same: any deviation from the antiracist framework is an ideological violation that cannot be tolerated. Hence, the white participant is told that they are racially illiterate, uninformed or misinformed, or simply speaking from opinion; their perspectives and worldviews are rendered invalid; and finally, it is insinuated that they are perpetuating racism.

But generalizing about whites in this manner is unhealthy and counterproductive, and is not the best way to bring about positive change. As a longtime Philadelphia schoolteacher and coach, I'd like to expand the conversation to include viewpoints from all races and ethnic backgrounds, and have a true open dialogue as opposed to a rigid ideological monologue. A tolerant, holistic approach to diversity, equity, and inclusion must be achieved to create the kinds of schools needed to educate all of America's children.

NOTES

1. Robin DiAngelo, *What Does It Mean To Be White?: Developing White Cultural Literacy Revised* (New York: Peter Lang, 2016), 158.
2. Ibid., 158.

Acknowledgments

The process involved with publishing a book is a complex one, and takes a team of dedicated individuals to do it right. As such, I'd like to thank the following people for their input, guidance, and contributions: Dr. Tom Koerner, Vice President and Publisher for Education Issues at Rowman and Littlefield, for his support and belief in the project; Jonathan Church, a writer and government economist, whose expertise in research methodology, philosophy, and whiteness studies gave this book that extra edge; Dr. Eugenia Krimmel, an education professor and ESL/bilingual education advisor at the Pennsylvania Department of Education, for her insightful input and suggestions; and the students, parents, and community of the School District of Philadelphia, whose pride, determination, and commitment to education have inspired me as a schoolteacher and coach for over two decades.

Finally, I'd like to thank my parents: Dr. Charles Paslay, a thirty-six-year veteran teacher, coach, and administrator with the School District of Philadelphia, whose feedback and support was invaluable; and Cheryl Paslay, my number one supporter, who helped me stay true to my vision and values.

Introduction

The One-Sided Conversation

In February of 2009, Eric Holder called America "a nation of cowards" for not talking about race.[1] Ten years later, through the efforts of antiracist educators like Robin DiAngelo, this conversation has finally come to fruition—although the "dialogue" on race is more of a monologue, where scholar-activists like DiAngelo lecture whites about their privilege in an inherently racist society, and where whites shake their heads and say, *Yes, I live in a world of white supremacy. Yes, my unconscious is loaded with implicit racial biases. Yes, America was founded on the backs of slaves. Yes, yes, yes . . .*

This is the only acceptable way for whites to engage in a "conversation" about race in 2020: to sincerely and enthusiastically swallow whole the teachings given them by experts on antiracism and white racial literacy. Silence and nonparticipation are not allowed. According to DiAngelo, "The racial status quo is not neutral; it's racist. Therefore, anything that works to maintain the status quo rather than challenge it maintains racism."[2]

In other words, white silence maintains racial comfort and equilibrium, which keeps white supremacy in place by failing to disrupt the racial hierarchy. So if you're white and don't want to appear closed-minded, you're obligated to join the conversation.

Disagreeing, of course, is strictly forbidden. Questioning, probing, challenging, or offering any alternative perspective outside of the approved antiracist school of thought is not an option; all disagreements are invalid, born out of ignorance and misinformation. If whites are persistent in their challenge, they may be told they suffer from "white fragility," a condition where whites become defensive or standoffish because they lack the endurance to withstand having their views on race confronted.[3]

Developed by DiAngelo, the theory is heavy on politics and light on science. As writer and noted white fragility critic Jonathan Church points out:

> Admittedly, DiAngelo draws upon a vast corpus of Whiteness Studies literature, has many years of experience in antiracist and multicultural education and has several publications to her name. Unfortunately, however, she also avoids debate, is reluctant to consider conflicting evidence and, most importantly, has a propensity to present her claims as doctrines to be instilled, rather than as hypotheses, which can be rigorously evaluated.[4]

Not included in the discussion on race are the costly consequences of putting politics before science. Although advocates of whiteness studies may genuinely strive for equity and social justice, the reality is that the discipline—in addition to bringing awareness to structural inequality—is having some unintended side effects on schools in America.

Research shows that anti-bias trainings aimed at bringing equality can hurt morale in schools. Besides the fact that these trainings are based on flawed implicit bias research, there is little evidence that they have any lasting effect on discriminatory behavior, and in some cases, may even provoke resentment among participants.[5]

The actions of New York City Schools Chancellor Richard Carranza in 2019 is a prime example. His use of anti-bias training to dismantle what he called "White Supremacy Culture" in schools sparked a major backlash, prompting administrators, teachers, and parents to call parts of the workshops "ugly and divisive."

Specifically, teachers were told by diversity consultants to "focus on black children over white ones," and one Jewish superintendent who described her family's Holocaust tragedies "was scolded and humiliated."[6] To make matters worse, four white New York City school district executives, who were demoted or stripped of duties under Carranza's administrative reorganization, sued the city, insisting he had created "an environment which is hostile toward whites."[7]

The dualistic concepts at the root of antiracism and white racial literacy—which view whites and people of color as oppressors/oppressed and advantaged/disadvantaged—can also have a negative impact on success in the classroom. As shown through a concept known as stereotype threat, the mere mention of race can directly affect academic achievement, graduation rates, and standardized test scores.[8]

Specifically, research shows that black students perform worse than whites on standardized tests when race is emphasized. When race is not emphasized, black students perform the same or better than whites. This indicates that academic performance can be harmed by the awareness that one's behavior might be viewed through the lens of race—and the bigger the focus on the identity group, the more vulnerable the students are to stereotype threat.[9] This is especially concerning when it comes to antiracist education, being that antiracism is hyperfocused on race and group identity.

Even more troubling, race-based discipline approaches—which employ antiracist concepts—have negatively impacted educational environments across America. In particular, the 2014 discipline guidelines put in place by the U.S. Department of Education and the Justice Department, which mandated that public schools limit suspensions and expulsions of black students, had numerous drawbacks.

A recent Fordham Institute study titled "Discipline Reform Through the Eyes of Teachers" revealed that educators in high-poverty schools reported "higher rates of verbal disrespect, physical fighting, and assault," and said a disorderly or unsafe environment made learning difficult. They also stated that discipline was inconsistent or inadequate, and that the recent decline in suspensions was at least partly explained by higher tolerance for misbehavior or increased underreporting. In short, the teachers surveyed—many of whom were people of color—felt that race-based discipline wasn't working, and actually made it harder for their students to learn.[10]

The shortcomings of whiteness studies do not stop there. For starters, the field is heavy on cause, and light on solution; the field is vague in that it strives for systemic reform which is at times nebulous and hard to track and translate into action; the field discounts the power of the individual's ability to change his or her life situation and the world around them; the field is based on zero-sum dichotomy rather than synergic unity; the field is at times patronizing and condescending, and seems to unconsciously reinforce white supremacy culture and the powerlessness of people of color; and most notably, the field refuses to acknowledge facts that are uncomfortable, or that run counter to their antiracist ideology.[11]

Because this book challenges whiteness studies and explores causes of inequality between whites and people of color outside of racism, it may prompt antiracist educators to accuse this book of perpetuating white supremacy culture; this book aims to do nothing of the sort. Those who truly care about truth and social change will read on with an open mind, as healthy debate and rigorous critique are the heart of the scientific method and the only path to true wisdom.

NOTES

1. Andy Barr, "Holder: 'Nation of Cowards' on Race," *Politico*, February 18, 2009, https://www.politico.com, (accessed November 30, 2019).

2. Robin DiAngelo, *What Does It Mean to Be White?: Developing White Cultural Literacy Revised* (New York: Peter Lang, 2016), 284.

3. Robin DiAngelo, *White Fragility: Why It's So Hard for White People to Talk about Racism* (Boston: Beacon Press, 2018), 11.

4. Jonathan Church, "The Theory of White Fragility: Scholarship or Proselytization?," *Areo*, January 25, 2019, https://areomagazine.com, (accessed November 30, 2019).

5. Frank Dobbin and Alexandra Kalev, "Why Diversity Programs Fail," *Harvard Business Review*, July–August, 2016, https://hbr.org (accessed November 30, 2019).

6. Susan Edelman, "Teachers Allegedly Told to Favor Black Students in 'Racial Equity' Training," *New York Post*, May 25, 2019, https://nypost.com (accessed November 30, 2019).

7. Susan Edelman, "Schools Chancellor Richard Carranza Accused of Demoting Admins Because They Were White," *New York Post*, May 18, 2019, https://nypost.com (accessed November 30, 2019).

8. "Stereotype Threat Widens Achievement Gap," *American Psychological Association*, July 15, 2006, https://www.apa.org, (accessed November 30, 2019).

9. Steve Stroessner and Catherine Good, "Stereotype Threat: An Overview," *Reducing Stereotype Threat*, http://www.reducingstereotypethreat.org/ (accessed December 3, 2019).

10. David Griffith and Adam Tyner, "Discipline Reform through the Eyes of Teachers," Thomas B. Fordham Institute, July 2019, https://fordhaminstitute.org, (accessed November 30, 2019).

11. Robin DiAngelo, *What Does It Mean to Be White?* (New York: Peter Lang, 2016).

Chapter One

The Tenets of Whiteness Studies

According to Wikipedia, America's foremost pop culture encyclopedia, "Whiteness studies is the study of the structures that produce white privilege, the examination of what whiteness is when analyzed as a race, a culture, and a source of systemic racism, and the exploration of other social phenomena generated by the societal compositions, perceptions and group behaviors of white people."[1]

Although whiteness studies can be traced all the way back to the writings of W. E. B. Du Bois, its contemporary emergence as a scholarly discipline began in the late 1980s and early 1990s, and its rise is usually associated with the highly influential article, "White Privilege: Unpacking the Invisible Knapsack," written by Peggy McIntosh in 1987.[2] The article was one of the first to view racism not as "individual acts of meanness," but as "invisible systems conferring dominance" on whites, and went on to list twenty-six specific ways in which white people enjoy a societal privilege over people of color. McIntosh centered her piece around the question: "Having described [white privilege], what will I do to lessen or end it?"[3]

Whiteness studies' mission to *end* privilege is notable, in that it operates from a zero-sum mentality. It doesn't aim to analyze whiteness to see why it's supposedly so dominant, or why it's led to all these privileges or advantages; it doesn't aim to reproduce these attributes. It doesn't ask the question: *what characteristics are at the heart of whiteness so we can replicate and share them?* It asks: *how can we disrupt or dismantle whiteness? How can we end it? How can we get whites to disrupt or dismantle themselves?*

At its core, whiteness studies is really a battle to define and control whiteness itself, given that the discipline views whiteness as property and a position of status.[4] One way whiteness studies aims to do this is by associating whiteness with oppression and structural racism. By redefining "racism" to mean inherent white privilege and oppression, *all* whites become guilty by default, even those whites who are caring people free from discrimination. Thus "whiteness" becomes "racism," which ultimately transforms the property of whiteness into the commodity of racism, and enables the politically oriented whiteness studies movement to usurp whiteness to use and redistribute as it sees fit.

The discipline, however, is not without its critics. "Whiteness has become a blank screen onto which those who claim to analyze it can project their own meanings," American historian Eric Arnesen concluded in 2001 after assessing the utility of whiteness studies for American historians.[5] Weakness in methodology, he argued, made it practically worthless, as did arbitrary and inconsistent definitions. The science behind whiteness studies in 2020 is still a point of contention, as are its fundamental tenets.

In 2009, researchers from the University of Minnesota and Augustana College published a paper called, "An Empirical Assessment of Whiteness Theory: Hidden from How Many?," which analyzed data from a national survey to offer an empirical assessment of the core theoretical tenets of whiteness studies. Although their aim wasn't to define whiteness studies itself, the tenets described in the study can serve as a good foundation for the discipline.

Simply stated, whiteness studies can be viewed as being concerned with the supposed invisibility of white identity (that whites don't see themselves as having a race, or that race doesn't matter); the understanding of white privilege (whether or not whites are aware of their so-called privileged status in society); and the belief in colorblindness and individualism (ideals that may hide both white identity and privilege).[6] Ultimately, the aim of whiteness studies is to make whites in society aware that they indeed have a race, that this race gives them a privilege over people of color, and that believing in colorblindness and individualism—luxuries not afforded non-whites—is actually perpetuating racism and white supremacy.

Central to whiteness studies is political activism. As DiAngelo states, whiteness studies "begin with the premise that racism and white privilege exist in both traditional and modern forms, and rather than work to prove its existence, work to reveal it," making the discipline more about forwarding a political narrative than using science to prove it.[7]

Nowhere is this more apparent than the theory of white racial identity development (WRID), which is political indoctrination at its core. Although there are multiple white identity theorists who've developed popular WRID models, each conform to a basic five- or six-step linear process where whites evolve from colorblind people unaware of race, to politically and socially active people who pledge to end white privilege and white supremacy.[8]

"White Racial Identity and Anti-Racist Education: A Catalyst for Change," by Sandra M. Lawrence and Beverly Daniel Tatum, is a useful model for understanding WRID, and incorporates a six-step approach.[9] Stage one is "Contact," where whiteness and its privileges remain invisible because of white isolation and are rarely acknowledged or reflected upon. Stage two is "Disintegration," marked by a new awareness of race and racism, usually precipitated by a heightened interaction with people of color or a new knowledge of white privilege and the systematic oppression of racial minorities.

Stage three is "Reintegration," where feelings of guilt and denial are transformed into fear and anger toward people of color, causing whites to "blame the victim" because they are unable to deal with the uncomfortable realities of racism. Stage four is "Pseudoindependence," marked by an intellectual understanding of racism as institutional and systematic, where whites assume a greater personal responsibility to dismantle privilege and oppression, and where they may seek to distance themselves from other whites in an attempt to come out of isolation and form more relationships with people of color.

Stage five is "Immersion/Emersion," where whites begin to accept their privilege and actively seek out allies to help them work against racism. And stage six is "Autonomy," where whites fully internalize their white identity development, and embrace a lifelong commitment to antiracist activity and ongoing self-examination.

One interesting note is that two highly influential models of WRID were developed and authored by women of color. Janet E. Helms, an African American psychologist and researcher known for her study of ethnic minority issues, first presented her theoretical WRID model in 1984, a model that is by far the most discussed and researched in the psychological literature.[10] In the 1990s psychologist and scholar Beverly Daniel Tatum, whose critically acclaimed and widely popular book *Why Are All the Black Kids Sitting Together in the Cafeteria?* thoroughly analyzed white racial identity development, presented her own educational model of WRID with Sandra M. Lawrence, which is referenced above.

The fact that Helms and Tatum are women of color is noteworthy in that this lays bare the fundamental double standard at the heart of whiteness studies and antiracism, which preaches that it's acceptable for racial minorities to critically analyze whiteness and the behaviors of white people, but not the other way around.

DiAngelo writes that only people of color can accurately analyze racism, and that whites—because of their privileged status in a white supremacist society—have no ability to be objective about racial matters. In *What Does It Mean To Be White?: Developing White Racial Literacy Revised*, DiAngelo writes about whites being "racially arrogant":

> Because of white social, economic, and political power within a white supremacist culture, whites are in the position to legitimize people of color's asser-

tions of racism. Yet whites are the least likely to see, understand, or be invested in validating those assertions and being honest about their consequences. This leads whites to claim that they disagree with perspectives that challenge their worldview when, in fact, they don't understand the perspective—thus confusing not understanding with not agreeing. The issue is that we don't understand racism. Declaring that we don't agree presumes that we are in an informed position that qualifies our disagreement.[11]

In essence, whites cannot disagree with people of color concerning matters of race and racism, as people of color—by virtue of their oppressed status in society—are much more aware and experienced in dealing with these issues. Likewise, whites are not permitted to question or challenge the established ideologies of whiteness studies or antiracism, as "informed knowledge and opinions are not the same."[12] This ultimately creates an awkward double standard in American classrooms and professional development trainings, where whites are judged and held to different standards than people of color.

MULTICULTURALISM VS. ANTIRACISM

To understand whiteness studies, one must first understand antiracist education. Addressing racism as a system of unequal power between whites and people of color, antiracism emerged as dissatisfaction grew with multicultural education, which only superficially dealt with the processes that create and perpetuate racism. As University of South Dakota sociologist Jack Niemonen wrote in his 2007 paper after doing an exhaustive analysis of 160 peer-reviewed journal articles on the subject:

> Generally, antiracist education is understood as a set of pedagogical, curricular, and organizational strategies that hope to promote racial equality by identifying, then eliminating, white privilege. Inspired by the principles of Paulo Freire, it employs the language of critique. One of its strengths, it is claimed, is the ability to move beyond prejudice and discrimination as a problem to be corrected in individuals in order to examine critically how institutional structures support racist practices economically, politically, and culturally.[13]

While multicultural education is relatively polite and mannerly—focusing on racial harmony and unity while celebrating diversity and cultural differences—antiracist education, by contrast, is at times blunt and unconcerned with being courteous, harmonious, or unifying. As DiAngelo stated in the white fragility webinar hosted by the Association of Delaware Valley Independent Schools in March of 2020, "niceness is not antiracism. . . . In fact, a culture of niceness is like a thick, thick blanket holding racism in place."[14]

Angelina E. Castagno's book, *The Price of Nice: How Good Intentions Maintain Educational Inequity*, reinforces this theme. As stated on the book jacket, "Niceness, as a raced, gendered, and classed set of behaviors, functions both as a shield to save educators from having to do the hard work of dismantling inequity and as a disciplining agent for those who attempt or even consider disrupting structures and ideologies of dominance."[15]

Antiracism is meant to draw attention to systemic inequality, and part of its design is to confront and even provoke whites into facing what they supposedly ignore—white privilege, institutional racism, and the perpetuation of these things through colorblindness and individualism. To draw an analogy from the American Civil Right movement, multiculturalism is Martin Luther King, and antiracism is Malcolm X—the former based on unity, love, and peaceful protest, the latter based on provocation, agitation, and the mantra "by any means necessary."

While King was content to wait for progress and to even turn the other cheek, Malcolm X refused to have a nine-inch knife pulled only six inches out of his back; critical race theory, which underpins antiracism, began as social justice advocates grew tired of patiently waiting for advances promised by the Civil Rights movement. As Niemonen states:

> Antiracist educators paint a picture of social reality in which battle lines are drawn, the enemy identified, and the victims sympathetically portrayed. Absolved of responsibility, the victims had domination, exploitation, and exclusion forced upon them. Here antiracist education distinguishes between "good" whites and "bad" whites.[16]

Simply stated, antiracist education is indoctrination; its ideologies are not open to discussion or debate. It's all or nothing: whites either get "woke" and pledge to end systemic white privilege by becoming antiracists, or perpetuate white supremacy by remaining silent. According to Niemonen, "antiracist educators justify pedagogical techniques that are coercive because bad whites aren't willing to change, or they reject the antiracist framework outright. As enemies, they defend a discredited white culture that claims supremacy."[17]

Although antiracist education tends to draw battle lines between woke and non-woke whites, antiracism still views general whiteness as racist and oppressive by default. According to Niemonen:

> Racism is an epistemology that privileges Eurocentric values, beliefs, and practices. It is the normative framework that defines "whiteness" as the standard by which to evaluate others. Racism is a set of institutionally embedded exclusionary practices that create, and then reproduce, socioeconomic status attainment disparities, including tracking in schools and discrimination in hiring. It is an aversion to critiquing the ideologies that justify existing arrange-

ments, such as equality of opportunity and meritocracy. Racism is manifested in opposition to race-targeted programs, such as affirmative action. Sometimes it is likened to distorted thinking, impaired consciousness, or a cancer on society.[18]

Comparing racism to cancer is an interesting analogy. There are two general ways to fight cancer: cancer awareness, and cancer research. Awareness is political, and involves spreading the message of the cause. The second is science, which entails analyzing the disease to find a cure. Whiteness studies and antiracism are both based on raising awareness—a kind of self-promotion that generates more awareness of whiteness studies and antiracism, which in turn forward the politics of these movements. There is no analysis of what makes whiteness so dominant, or how, for hundreds of years all over the globe, whiteness was able to enjoy such advantages and privileges. How did whiteness pull such a thing off for so long?

The answer, according to antiracists, is tragically circular: white supremacy happens because of white supremacy, and structural racism happens because of structural racism. Period. No need for further inquiry or analysis; even suggesting that inequality can be solved by means other than addressing racism is blasphemous, as racism is the *one and only cause* of racial disparities in the world.[19] For antiracists, the only solution is antiracism, the goal of which is to identify, then eliminate, white privilege.

Curiously, antiracists tend to discredit the scientific method as racist, and insist that Western epistemology is nothing more than domination by Eurocentric white men. As researcher Jack Niemonen writes in his critical assessment of antiracist education, "Antiracist educators reject the conception of research as advancement of knowledge for its own sake in favor of one that says that research must be judged in terms of its contribution to political projects that eliminate racism. As a consequence, questions of reality or fact can be adjudicated on moral or political grounds."[20]

Antiracism is not a sociological grounded, empirically based account of race in America. Unlike multiculturalism, it seeks to go beyond celebrating racial diversity to provoke whites into acknowledging their privileged status in an inherently racist white supremacist society. It's rooted in identity politics and is in essence, like whiteness studies, political activism. Whether or not America's classrooms should be used for political indoctrination—and how this indoctrination is impacting both the educational skills and attitudes of America's young people and teachers—will be explored later in this book.

WHITE PRIVILEGE AND WHITE FRAGILITY

At the heart of whiteness studies and antiracist education is a concept known as "white privilege." Although a variation of the term goes back as far as

1837, when an issue of William Lloyd Garrison's abolitionist newspaper *The Liberator* published a resolution demanding colored men be given "the privilege of whites,"[21] the contemporary term is usually attributed to the 1987 Peggy McIntosh article, "White Privilege: Unpacking the Invisible Knapsack."[22] The term is as recognizable as it is contentious. As Teaching Tolerance senior writer Cory Collins states:

> White privilege is—perhaps most notably in this era of uncivil discourse—a concept that has fallen victim to its own connotations. The two-word term packs a double whammy that inspires pushback. 1) The word white creates discomfort among those who are not used to being defined or described by their race. And 2) the word privilege, especially for poor and rural white people, sounds like a word that doesn't belong to them—like a word that suggests they have never struggled.[23]

As Collins explains in his article, white privilege is *not* the idea that whites have not struggled, or that everything a white person has accomplished is unearned. Generally speaking, white privilege is associated with the understanding that whites have a greater access to societal power and resources than do people of color. Like the progressive perspective of racism, white privilege is structural, and an individual good/bad binary does not apply. In other words, white people can be kind and generous human beings while still having a so-called privilege.

Collins identifies the manifestations of white privilege in three areas: white privilege as the "power of normal," where society instinctively caters to the needs of whites, such as "flesh colored" Band-Aids, Eurocentric hair care products and grocery store items; white privilege as the "power of the benefit of the doubt," where whites are less likely to be followed in a store, interrogated and searched by police, or denied an application for a loan; and white privilege as the "power of accumulated power," where whites enjoy substantially higher net incomes, educational attainment, and access to health care than do people of color.[24]

From an antiracist framework, the first step in eliminating white privilege is recognition. This entails getting whites to "check their privilege," which is a basic acknowledgment of the ways in which whites have better—and in some cases, *unearned*—access to power and resources in society. Once whites take this first step, they can then use their so-called privilege to benefit people of all races.

As is the heart of whiteness studies and antiracism in general, the bulk of these solutions are *political*, and involve fully embracing the ideologies of the cause, and of pledging to forward the narrative by educating others and convincing them to get politically and socially active. Similarly, the concept of ending white privilege is zero-sum, and calls for the disruption and/or removal of something in order to bring about so-called justice—not the addition or adaption of something. As Jonathan Church writes in his article, "The Problem I Have with the Concept of White Privilege":

> White-privilege is often deployed in conversation in a tone that implies it should be taken away. Hence the phrase "check your privilege." But checking privilege may not always be the morally-sound antidote. If we are talking about rights rather than privileges, then the focus of the discussion should be how to cultivate a society in which black people take for granted the rights that white people take for granted. Rather than "check your privilege", the goal is a society in which cops give both the white and black kid the benefit of the doubt, rather than a society in which the cop refuses to give the benefit of the doubt to the white person simply because he does not give the benefit of the doubt to the black person (as if two wrongs make a right). The issue is to expand rights to those who don't have it, not take it away from those who have it.[25]

Outside of racism, the "check your privilege" approach doesn't aim to analyze how or why privileges in society exist, or attempt to directly supply people of color with the means or methods to help them partake in these benefits. In fact, suggesting that people of color may need some form of education or skill building is known as cultural deficit theory, a concept lambasted by antiracists as oppressive and perpetuating white supremacy, and of ultimately "blaming the victim."

Ironically, it appears as though antiracists believe that white supremacy is only going to end when white people decide it will end, and when whites sufficiently unpack their privilege and allow people of color to have equal access to resources; it doesn't take a whiteness scholar to see that this isn't very empowering to people of color.

In addition to the zero-sum quality of white privilege, the misleading nature of the term leaves it open to misrepresentation by politicians and the news media. During the Democratic presidential debate on CNN in July of 2019, Kirsten Gillibrand spoke of her duty to lecture suburban white women about their "white privilege," stating that "when their child has a car that breaks down, and he knocks on someone's door for help, and the door opens, and the help is given, it's his whiteness that protects him from being shot."[26]

Gillibrand's suggestion that whites are opening their doors and randomly shooting black teens for no good reason further distorts the concept of "white privilege," and adds even more fuel to the political fire. Yet her words were met with thunderous applause during the debate, and replayed in the media for several days. Too often, these distortions are echoed by young adults in educational settings, prompting students of color to be less trustworthy of whites and provoking within them feelings of resentment.

But like so much with antiracism, disagreeing with this kind of ideology is not an option. Those who deny their privilege will be told they suffer from "white fragility," a condition where whites supposedly become extremely fragile when they are faced with talking about race. According to Robin DiAngelo, whose white fragility theory has become one of the most influential ideas about racism in America, whites consider a challenge to their worldviews on race a challenge to their worth as a person. As she explains in her book, *White Fragility*:

> The smallest amount of racial stress is intolerable—the mere suggestion that being white has meaning often triggers a range of defense responses. These include emotions such as anger, fear, and guilt and behaviors such as argumentation, silence, and withdraw from the stress-inducing situation. These responses work to reinstate white equilibrium as they repel the challenge, return our racial comfort, and maintain our dominance within the racial hierarchy.[27]

Not that DiAngelo has done the rigorous hypothesis testing and quantitative measurement necessary to prove any of this. As writer and noted white fragility critic Jonathan Church noted, "the theory of white fragility is so superficial—and so laden with bugs, glitches, defects and factual errors—that it is a wonder it has not yet self-destructed."[28] Incredibly, DiAngelo has no problem speaking in generalities, and admits to being "quite comfortable generalizing," because "social life is patterned and predictable in measurable ways."[29]

So generalize she does, especially about how whites are racially illiterate and fragile. And when whites challenge DiAngelo's assessment of their supposed fragility—or dare to offer solutions different from those approved by the antiracist school of thought—DiAngelo dismisses them as ignorant and uninformed.

"RACISM" AND "WHITE SUPREMACY"

Antiracist educators, working within the field of whiteness studies, have successfully incorporated their ideologies into mainstream society by strategically redefining the terms "racism" and "white supremacy" to fit their progressive antiracist narrative.

Traditionally, "racism" is understood as a kind of personal prejudice or discrimination against an individual based on race, which negatively judges a person by the color of their skin. Racism is "bad" and employed by "racists"—ignorant, uneducated, or otherwise insensitive people whose belief in stereotypes causes them to act out against those of other races, ethnicities, or nationalities, sometimes in aggressive or violent ways. According to Merriam-Webster, racism is "a belief that race is the primary determinant of human traits and capacities and that racial differences produce an inherent superiority of a particular race."[30]

Similarly, "white supremacy" is the belief that whites are biologically superior to all other races, and that whites have fundamental rights not afforded people of color. White supremacy is a socially condemned behavior employed by "white supremacists," individuals who are often members of violent hate groups such as the Aryan Nation or the Ku Klux Klan. According to Merriam-Webster, a white supremacist is "a person who believes that the white race is inherently superior to other races and that white people should have control over people of other races."[31]

Using these mainstream definitions as a reference, there are very few whites who would knowingly accept being labeled a racist or a white supremacist. In fact, the accusations of racism and white supremacy are so damning, they regularly end the careers of celebrities and public officials; the 2018 racist tweet by Roseanne Barr which abruptly ended the comeback of her sitcom, and the "blackface" controversy which prompted the firing of Megyn Kelly from NBC News and the resignation of Florida Secretary of State Mike Ertel, are several examples.

Indeed, there is no shortage of racism and white supremacy in the news media—stories about hate crime hoaxes like the one attributed to Jussie Smollett, or racially motivated mass shootings like the 2019 El Paso massacre by so-called white nationalist Patrick Crusius which killed twenty-two people and injured twenty-four others.

Yet incredibly, antiracist educators have successfully managed to redefine the terms "racism" and "white supremacy" to fit their ideology, and to forward a narrative rooted in identity politics. In her book, *What Does It Mean To Be White?*, Robin DiAngelo defines "racism" as structural as opposed to individual, a form of oppression in which one racial group dominates another. She writes:

> Racism is more than race prejudice. Anyone across any race can have race prejudice. But *racism* is a macro-level social system that whites control and use to the advantage of whites as a group. Thus all whites are collectively implicated in this system.[32]

She goes on to explain that only whites can be racist, because whites have collective social and institutional power over people of color. In addition, *all* whites are racist, because all whites collectively benefit from racism via white privilege. She insists the mainstream definition of racism, which she calls a "good/bad binary," is false because racism is not personal but systemic, and that you can still perpetuate racism and be a good person.[33]

DiAngelo defines "white supremacy" as "the term used to capture the all-encompassing centrality and assumed superiority of people defined and perceived as white, and the practices based on this assumption." She writes:

> White supremacy does not refer to individual white people per se and their individual intentions, but to a political-economic social system of domination. This system is based on the historical and current accumulation of structural power that privileges, centralizes, and elevates white people as a group.[34]

This progressive version of "white supremacy" started to gain traction in 1997 with the publication of Charles M. Mills's book *The Racial Contract*, where he describes white supremacy as "the unnamed political system that has made the modern world what it is today."[35] He argues that while white supremacy is a political system that has shaped Western thought for hundreds of years, it remains invisible—a phenomenon some claim is the root of its power; interestingly, a good portion of Charles Mills's work, which deals with oppositional political theory, is based in politics.

Through the efforts of scholar-activists like Mills and DiAngelo, the new progressive definition of "white supremacy" is steadily gaining popularity, especially in education. "What Happened When My School Started to Dismantle White Supremacy Culture," a blog article published in *Education Week* in July of 2019, describes how a "brave staff" spent a majority of the 2018–2019 school year unpacking White Supremacy Culture at Visitacion Valley Middle School in the San Francisco Unified school district.[36]

In the fall of 2019, New York City Schools Chancellor Richard Carranza used anti-bias training to dismantle what he called "White Supremacy Culture," although this training sparked a major backlash prompting administrators, teachers, and parents to call the workshops "ugly and divisive."[37]

Indeed, workshops teaching that all whites perpetuate racism and white supremacy by default might prompt some in the education community to call such approaches divisive, especially in light of the fact that many parents, teachers, administrators, and students only know racism and white supremacy by their mainstream definitions. And even if America's education communities got up to speed on the revised antiracist definitions, there's a good chance many would be shocked by the progressive interpretations; indeed, this is already happening in my own school district in Philadelphia.

Still, antiracists within the field of whiteness studies could very easily end this confusion by replacing these terms with words not associated with hate crime, mass shootings, personal prejudice, and all-round abhorrent behavior. Antiracists could do what the organizers of ARC did in 1992, when they formally changed their name from the "Association for Retarded Citizens of the United States," to "The ARC of the United States."

Perhaps the terms "racism" and "white supremacy" could be replaced with phrases less offensive and more reflective of their intended meaning, like "macro-dominance" and "Euro-elitism." This would still shine a light on these so-called systems of oppression and end their supposed invisibility, while not attaching to them the overly negative and misleading connotations mentioned above.

Although "macro-dominance" and "Euro-elitism" don't pack nearly the same political punch—and would lessen the ability of antiracists to use racism as a commodity and source of power—changing the terms would force proponents of whiteness studies to approach social and educational equality from a more honest standpoint, and would ultimately be less confusing and divisive for teachers, students, parents, and administrators.

COLORBLINDNESS AND INDIVIDUALISM

A major theoretical tenant of whiteness studies is the white person's belief in colorblindness and individualism, and how these beliefs serve to both obscure and perpetuate white privilege and institutional racism. As with the terms racism and white supremacy, colorblindness and individualism have been redefined within the fields of whiteness studies to fit a progressive antiracist narrative.

Traditionally, colorblindness is a positive—a way of viewing the world not through the superficial lens of race and skin color, but through a deeper perspective, one centered on universal human values like love, compassion, tolerance, honesty, and friendship. Often times, the concept of colorblindness is associated with Martin Luther King's "I Have a Dream" speech, where he famously stated that he dreamed of a time when his children would be judged not by the color of their skin but by the content of their character.

But the concept of colorblindness has been completely overtaken and redefined by antiracists, so much so that its meaning has literally been inverted and turned on its head—going from a positive that society should strive to attain to a negative that it should guard against. Within the field of whiteness studies, the concept is now known as "colorblind racism," and antiracist educators now call for people not to be colorblind, but to be "color-bold."

According to DiAngelo, colorblind racism is "pretending that we don't notice race or that race has no meaning. This pretense denies racism and thus holds it in place."[38] DiAngelo's definition ties in directly with the essential question of her book on white racial literacy *What Does It Mean To Be White?*, which asks, "What does it mean to be white in a society that proclaims race meaningless, yet is deeply divided by race?"[39]

But there's a fundamental problem with both the essential question of DiAngelo's book and with her definition of colorblind racism. According to "An Empirical Assessment of Whiteness Theory: Hidden from How Many?", which used data from the American Mosaic Project to test the hypotheses developed in the paper, race *does* matter to white people, as 74 percent of white Americans surveyed—almost three-fourths—said that their racial identity was either "very important" or "somewhat important."

Likewise, 72 percent of nonwhites said it was "very important," and an additional 17 percent said it was "somewhat important."[40] And according to a 2016 Pew Research study on America's views on race and inequality, 31 percent of whites admitted that being white made it easier for them to succeed, while 53 percent of whites said more must be done to bring about racial equality in America.[41]

It's not that the majority of whites think race *doesn't* matter, it's that they think it *shouldn't* matter; there's a major difference between these two concepts. Nearly all Americans are aware of race, especially in light of the news media's obsession with race and racism on television, in newspapers, and on the internet.

Granted, some whites may not always be aware of the advantages race gives them in their daily life, or the ways in which race may disadvantage people of color in certain situations. But the notion that whites believe race doesn't matter is cause for further study and investigation, as it seems hard to believe that in 2020, whites aren't aware that race has meaning, and that race is often used in various situations in both positive and negative ways.

True colorblindness isn't "pretending we don't notice race or that race has no meaning" as DiAngelo claims. Traditional colorblindness is the filtering out of the superficial characteristics of eye shape, hair texture, and skin tone, and of connecting and interacting with others via the universal human values of love, kindness, honesty, tolerance, respect, and compassion. If all people learned to do as much, not just casually but with the very core of their beings, the world would be a different place. Racism, prejudice, discrimination, and all manner of social injustice would begin to subside.

When most whites say they don't see color, they don't mean color doesn't matter, they mean it *shouldn't* matter. Of course they are aware of race and culture, and that these things have an impact on people's lives, but they're not *hyperfocused* on color in the present moment; when a white coach in an all-black setting is completely absorbed with coaching his athletes, he can sometimes forget he is the only white person there.

It is this disingenuous redefining of colorblindness that is most concerning in whiteness studies and antiracism. In essence, it's taking a positive outlook by well-meaning people, white and people of color alike, and twisting it into something negative that can be used to forward a political ideology—or to discredit those who have an alternative perspective.

It's one thing to take terms which already have negative connotations—like "racism" and "white supremacy"—and tweak them to fit a political narrative. But it's quite another to take a positive term like "colorblindness" and rebrand it to mean the total opposite of what it was intended to mean;

again, this is not healthy for education, and is causing confusion, bitterness, and mistrust among learning communities.

A major goal of antiracist educators within the field of whiteness studies is to level the playing field and end systemic racial disparities. The purpose behind creating the term "colorblind racism" is clearly to make whites as equally aware of race and racism as nonwhites are, which will in effect "bear witness" to injustice, and help bring an end to it.

But what happens then? Once everybody's sufficiently aware of the ugly consequences of race, then what? Logic would suggest the next step would entail teaching people *not* to judge people by the color of their skin, and to connect and interact with them as fellow humans instead of treating them as "others." In other words, it would be time to circle back and employ colorblindness. As T. S. Eliot said, *We shall not cease from exploration, and the end of all our exploring will be to arrive where we started and know the place for the first time.*

Still, there's a more cynical perspective as to why the field of whiteness studies doesn't take the direct path and preach traditional colorblindness, and that's because indoctrinating society to be hyperaware of race is helping keep race at the forefront—right where antiracists need it to be. Race and racism are indeed invaluable when it comes to identity politics, so teaching Americans to be "blind" to it makes no sense politically, and would negatively impact racism as a commodity and source of power.

As for the concept of individualism, this is tied in closely with colorblindness, and can be understood much of the same way. According to DiAngelo, individualism is "the ideology that we are all unique, therefore categories such as race have no meaning and provide no more or no less opportunities. Thus success or failure is not a consequence of social structures but of individual character."[42] DiAngelo goes on to explain that individualism denies white privilege and institutional racism, hides the accumulation of wealth, denies collective socialization and the power of the dominant culture to shape social perspectives, functions as "neo-colorblindness" and reproduces the myth of meritocracy, and makes collective action difficult.[43]

Like with the criticism of colorblindness, this is a disingenuous representation of the concept, and a complete overgeneralization; interestingly, as mentioned previously, DiAngelo has no problem speaking in generalities, and admits to being "quite comfortable generalizing," because "social life is patterned and predictable in measurable ways."[44] Generalizations are only permitted, of course, when they forward an antiracist ideology. Any generalization that might suggest that disparities between the races are due to things other than simply racism—like out-of-wedlock birth, for example—would not only be attacked for being an overgeneralization, but would be diagnosed as a clear example of aversive racism.

Which is exactly why a concept like individualism cannot exist within an antiracist framework: because the idea acknowledges that individuals have some measure of independence outside of institutional or societal structures—emphasis on the word *some*; individualism assumes a minimum level of personal responsibility, and accepts that choices have consequences.

According to Merriam-Webster, individualism is "a doctrine that the interests of the individual are or ought to be ethically paramount." A secondary definition by Merriam-Webster is, "a theory maintaining the political and economic independence of the individual and stressing individual initiative, action, and interests."[45] Nowhere within these definitions is race mentioned, or whether race has meaning or provides more or less opportunities. These adaptions come wholly out of the politics of antiracism, and once again twist the traditional concept into a progressive version unfamiliar to many in mainstream America.

Thus, a positive becomes a negative, and develops into an idea with a hyperfocus on race. Abandoned are the notions of freedom, independence, and the ability to shape the course and quality of your life—conditions that, although limited in certain situations by home environment, social class, and institutional inequality—are more readably available in America than most countries in the world.

Tragically, with the discrediting of individualism within the whiteness studies movement, our nation's children of color are now being taught that it's not possible to be the captain of your own ship, and that it's no use trying to man the rudder, because a racist society will ultimately make you ride along somewhere in the bowels below deck.

IMPACT VS. INTENT

There's a growing movement within whiteness studies to "think impact, not intent."

"I think intentions are irrelevant," DiAngelo admitted in an interview with *Teaching Tolerance*. "It's nice to know you had good intentions, but the impact of what you did was harmful. And we need to let go of our intentions and attend to the impact, to focus on that."[46]

Because only people of color can accurately analyze racism, and that whites—because of their privileged status in a white supremacist society—have no ability to be objective about racial matters, a white person's intentions can be rendered meaningless if a person of color interprets them as racist. This perspective is effectively gaining ground due to two concepts being actively promoted by antiracist educators within the fields of whiteness studies: implicit bias, and microaggressions; the notion of implicit bias in particular underpins a very large majority of antiracism and whiteness studies ideology, serving as the fundamental basis for many of the theories developed by these schools of thought.

Unfortunately, as will be detailed in chapter 2, the actual science behind implicit bias and microaggressions is relatively weak. Much of the data behind implicit bias—a person's so-called unconscious discriminatory attitudes which directly influence their behavior—is based on the Implicit Association Test (IAT), co-created by Harvard University psychology chair Mahzarin Banaji, University of Washington researcher Anthony Greenwald, and University of Virginia scholar Brian Nosek.

Supposedly, the IAT can accurately measure unconscious bias and therefore real-world behavior. However, research continues to show, in the words of *New York Magazine* writer Jesse Singal, "that there's very little evidence to support that claim that the IAT meaningfully predicts anything." Singal writes:

> In fact, the test is riddled with statistical problems—problems severe enough that it's fair to ask whether it is effectively "misdiagnosing" the millions of people who have taken it, the vast majority of whom are likely unaware of its very serious shortcomings. There's now solid research published in a top journal strongly suggesting the test *cannot* even meaningfully predict individual behavior. And if the test can't predict individual behavior, it's unclear exactly what it *does* do or why it should be the center of so many conversations and programs geared at fighting racism.[47]

The science behind microaggressions, defined as "the myriad slights and insults that people of color endure on a daily basis, most often from well-intentioned whites,"[48] is just as dubious. In 2017, Emory University psychology professor Scott O. Lilienfeld published a paper titled, "Microaggressions: Strong Claims, Inadequate Evidence," which argued that the microaggression research program (MRP) "is far too underdeveloped on the conceptual and methodological fronts to warrant real-world application."

The paper also recommended the abandonment of the term "microaggression," and called for "a moratorium on microaggression training programs and publicly distributed microaggression lists pending research to address the MRP's scientific limitations."[49]

This hasn't stopped the whiteness studies movement from using implicit bias and microaggressions to forward their narrative on racism and white supremacy, however. Despite the absence of hard data, antiracist educators continue to use both concepts as a means to focus on impact over intent, claiming the unconscious biases and microaggressions of well-meaning whites are causing them to perpetuate racism despite their intentions to do otherwise.

So when a situation arises between a white individual and a person of color, and the person of color feels slighted or victimized by racist behavior, the intention of the white person doesn't matter; it's just the *impact* of the white person's behavior that counts. Furthermore, because whites have no racial objectivity, only the person of color can determine if the behavior was insulting or racist, as there's no co-creation or co-responsibility between the races when it comes to antiracism; the fact that a person of color may be overly sensitive, touchy, or may have misinterpreted the white person's behavior doesn't matter.

Focusing on impact over intent is not without controversy. In April of 2018, two black men were removed from a Starbucks in the Rittenhouse Square section of Philadelphia by police for refusing to make a purchase. The men asked to use the bathroom and were told by a Starbucks manager that the restrooms were for paying customers only, and were asked to leave. The two men, who were apparently meeting a friend for a business meeting, didn't leave or buy anything.[50]

They sat down at a table, disregarding the manager, who was a white female, so she called the police; because of a loitering problem in the Rittenhouse Starbucks, managers were apparently instructed to reserve the store for paying customers only. "Hi, I have two gentlemen in my café that are refusing to make a purchase or leave," the manager said, according to the 911 call. "I'm at the Starbucks at 18th and Spruce."[51]

The police came and respectfully tried to explain to the men, for nearly fifteen minutes, that they needed to leave or be charged with trespassing. According to Philadelphia Police Commissioner Richard Ross, the police gave the men three chances to leave, but they didn't move.[52] Finally, the two men were escorted out in handcuffs, but not arrested.

The incident was captured on cellphone video by a woman in the store, who then put it up on the internet. The video went viral, prompting a personal apology from Starbucks CEO Kevin Johnson, and causing the closing of 8,000 stores for anti-bias training. The Rittenhouse Starbucks was soon boycotted and vandalized. The manager was quietly transferred to another store, and Philadelphia Police Commissioner Richard Ross soon caved to pressure and apologized for making a mistake. Later that month, Starbucks issued a new company policy that stated all were welcome at Starbucks—paying customers or not.

The ruling in the court of public opinion was that the Philadelphia police officers (one of whom was black) and the Starbucks manager were racist, if not consciously, unconsciously. They suffered from implicit bias, and their intentions didn't matter. Sure, the store manager was only following store policy at the time, and the police were only following the law in regard to loitering on private property, but it was the impact of their actions that truly counted; the two black men felt harassed and discriminated against, which is all that mattered.

Believing that the two black men could have respected the authority of the manager and purchased a cookie or cup of coffee for a few dollars or left the store was apparently unreasonable. Social justice advocates insisted that if the men would have been white, the manager would have left them alone; defenders of the manager and police insisted that if the men would have been white, their arrests would have gone unnoticed. There was no way of definitively proving any of this, except for the accusation of implicit bias, which was all that was needed to prove the manager and police guilty of racism.

The Philadelphia Starbucks example is only one of many situations were impact is overriding intent; in April of 2019, black R&B singer SZA said she was racially profiled at a Sephora store in Calabasas, prompting Sephora to close all of its U.S. stores for anti-bias training.[53] Although the impact of an individual's actions is clearly important, rendering intentions meaningless, as is the trend by antiracists, is no way to foster communication between races.

A more holistic approach, where whites and people of color interact as co-creators and share responsibility for effectively communicating, is needed to bridge the divide between different groups. Holding one group accountable over another, especially in situations where misperceptions can occur, is a recipe for further resentment and division.

RECOMMENDATIONS

1. Whiteness studies' mission should not be to *end* privilege, but to expand advantages to people of all races.

2. Antiracist educators should not employ pedagogical techniques that are coercive and rely on indoctrination, but should remain open to healthy debate—discussions that focus on racial harmony and unity while promoting multiculturalism and diversity in all areas of society.

3. Whiteness scholars should refrain from overgeneralizing and labeling entire groups of people, and the term "white supremacy" should no longer be used within the context of whiteness studies and antiracist education, given that the phrase has extremely negative connotations and is often misunderstood by the population at large; a more appropriate term must be developed to describe institutional and educational inequality, a term not commonly associated with hatred, violence, and fascism.

4. Similarly, all whites should not be accused of perpetuating "racism" by default; the redefining of "racism" to mean systemic dominance by whites, regardless of personal intentions and circumstance, is misguided. The good/bad binary of racism still exists in mainstream America, and whiteness scholars must respect this by developing new definitions that do not confuse or mislead students, parents, teachers, and the education community at large.

5. True colorblindness isn't "pretending we don't notice race or that race has no meaning." Traditional colorblindness is the filtering out of the superficial characteristics of eye shape, hair texture, and skin tone, and of connecting and interacting with others via the universal human values of love, kindness, honesty, tolerance, respect, and compassion. When most whites say they don't see color, they don't mean color doesn't matter, they mean it *shouldn't* matter.

6. Although the impact of an individual's actions is clearly important, rendering intentions meaningless, as is the trend by antiracists, is no way to foster communication between races. A more holistic approach, where whites and people of color interact as co-creators and share responsibility for effectively communicating, is needed to bridge the divide between different groups.

NOTES

1. "Whiteness Studies," Wikipedia, https://en.wikipedia.org/ (accessed December 31, 2019).
2. Peggy McIntosh, "White Privilege: Unpacking the Invisible Knapsack," *Peace and Freedom Magazine*, July/August, 1989, 10–12.
3. Ibid.
4. Robin DiAngelo, *What Does It Mean to Be White?: Developing White Cultural Literacy Revised* (New York: Peter Lang, 2016), 104–105.
5. Eric Arnesen, "Whiteness and the Historians' Imagination," *International Labor and Working-Class History*, No. 60 (Fall, 2001), pp. 3–32.
6. Douglas Hartmann, Joseph Gerteis, and Paul R. Croll, "An Empirical Assessment of Whiteness Theory: Hidden from How Many?," *Society for the Study of Social Problems*, Vol. 56, No. 3 (August 2009), pp. 403–424.
7. Robin DiAngelo, "White Fragility," *The International Journal of Critical Pedagogy*, Vol. 3, No. 3 (2011), http://libjournal.uncg.edu (accessed November 30, 2019).
8. Joseph G. Ponterotto, Shawn O. Utsey, and Paul B. Pedersen, *Preventing Prejudice: A Guide for Counselors, Educators, and Parents* (Thousand Oaks, CA: Sage Publications, 2006), 88–108.
9. Sandra M. Lawrence and Beverly Daniel Tatum, "White Racial Identity and Anti-Racist Education: A Catalyst for Change," Teaching for Change, https://www.teachingforchange.org (accessed December 31, 2019).
10. Joseph G. Ponterotto, Shawn O. Utsey, and Paul B. Pedersen, *Preventing Prejudice*, 88–108.
11. Robin DiAngelo, *What Does It Mean to Be White?* (New York: Peter Lang, 2016), 205–206.
12. Ibid., 20.
13. Jack Niemonen, "Antiracist Education in Theory and Practice: A Critical Assessment," *The American Sociologist*, Vol. 38, No. 2 (June 2007), pp. 159–177.
14. Robin DiAngelo, Ali Michael, and Toni Graves Williamson, "ADVIS Critical Conversations: White Fragility and Affinity Group Webinar," Association of Delaware Valley Independent Schools, March 12, 2020.
15. Angelina E. Castagno, *The Price of Nice: How Good Intentions Maintain Educational Inequity* (Minneapolis, MN: University of Minnesota Press, 2019).
16. Jack Niemonen, "Antiracist Education in Theory and Practice," 165–166.
17. Ibid., 166.
18. Ibid., 161.

19. Robin DiAngelo, *What Does It Mean to Be White?* (New York: Peter Lang, 2016), 132.
20. Jack Niemonen, "Antiracist Education," *The American Sociologist*, Vol. 38, No. 2 (June 2007), pp. 161.
21. Jacob Bennett, "White Privilege: A History of the Concept," History Thesis, Georgia State University Department of History, April 11, 2012, https://scholarworks.gsu.edu/ (accessed December 31, 2019).
22. Peggy McIntosh, "White Privilege," *Peace and Freedom Magazine*, July/August, 1989, 10–12.
23. Cory Collins, "What is White Privilege, Really?," *Teaching Tolerance*, Issue 60, Fall 2018, https://www.tolerance.org/magazine/fall-2018 (accessed December 31, 2019).
24. Ibid.
25. Jonathan Church, "The Problem I Have with the Concept of White Privilege," *The Good Men Project*, March 19, 2017, https://goodmenproject.com (accessed December 31, 2019).
26. "Democratic Debate Transcript: July 31, 2019," NBC News, July 31, 2019, https://www.nbcnews.com (accessed January 18, 2020).
27. Robin DiAngelo, *White Fragility: Why It's So Hard for White People to Talk about Racism* (Boston: Beacon Press, 2018), xiii.
28. Jonathan Church, "Whiteness Studies and the Theory of White Fragility Are Based on a Logical Fallacy," *Areo*, April 25, 2019, https://areomagazine.com (accessed November 30, 2019).
29. Robin DiAngelo, *White Fragility* (Boston: Beacon Press, 2018), 22.
30. "Racism," Merriam-Webster Online, https://www.merriam-webster.com (accessed December 31, 2019).
31. "White Supremacist," Merriam-Webster Online, https://www.merriam-webster.com (accessed December 31, 2019).
32. Robin DiAngelo, *What Does It Mean to Be White?* (New York: Peter Lang, 2016), 109.
33. Ibid., 23–24.
34. Ibid., 146.
35. Charles Mills, *The Racial Contract* (New York: Cornell University Press, 1997), 1.
36. Joe Truss, "What Happened When My School Started to Dismantle White Supremacy Culture," *Education Week*, July 18, 2019, https://www.edweek.org (accessed December 31, 2019).
37. Susan Edelman, "Teachers Allegedly Told to Favor Black Students in 'Racial Equity' Training," *New York Post*, May 25, 2019, https://nypost.com (accessed December 31, 2019).
38. Robin DiAngelo, *What Does It Mean to Be White?* (New York: Peter Lang, 2016), 130.
39. Ibid., 14.
40. Douglas Hartmann, Joseph Gerteis, and Paul R. Croll, "An Empirical Assessment of Whiteness Theory," *Society for the Study of Social Problems*, Vol. 56, No. 3 (August 2009), pp. 403–424.
41. "On Views of Race and Inequality, Blacks and Whites Are Worlds Apart," Pew Research Center, June 27, 2016, https://www.pewsocialtrends.org, (accessed December 31, 2019).
42. Robin DiAngelo, *What Does It Mean to Be White?* (New York: Peter Lang, 2016), 130.
43. Ibid., 195–200.
44. Robin DiAngelo, *White Fragility* (Boston: Beacon Press, 2018), 22.
45. "Individualism," Merriam-Webster Online, https://www.merriam-webster.com (accessed December 31, 2019).
46. Adrienne Van Der Valk and Anya Malley, "What's My Complicity? Talking White Fragility with Robin DiAngelo," *Teaching Tolerance*, Issue 62, Summer 2019, https://www.tolerance.org (accessed November 30, 2019).
47. Jesse Singal, "The Creators of the Implicit Association Test Should Get Their Story Straight," *Intelligencer*, December 5, 2017, http://nymag.com/intelligencer (Accessed December 31, 2019).
48. Robin DiAngelo, *What Does It Mean to Be White?* (New York: Peter Lang, 2016), 224.
49. Scott O. Lilienfeld, "Microaggressions: Strong Claims, Inadequate Evidence," *Perspectives on Psychological Science*, Vol. 12, No. 1 (2017), pp. 138–169.

50. Rob Tornoe, "What happened at Starbucks in Philadelphia?," *Philadelphia Inquirer*, April 16, 2018, https://www.inquirer.com (accessed December 31, 2019).

51. "Listen: Manager's 911 Call Before Arrest of 2 Black Men at Philly Starbucks," NBC10 Philadelphia, April 17, 2018, https://www.nbcphiladelphia.com (accessed December 31, 2019).

52. "Commissioner: Philadelphia Officer Did Not Want to Make Starbucks Arrest," Action News, 6ABC Philadelphia, April 16, 2018, https://6abc.com (accessed December 31, 2019).

53. Kate Taylor, "Sephora Will Temporarily Close All Its Stores on Wednesday," *Business Insider*, June 4, 2019, https://www.businessinsider.com (accessed December 31, 2019).

Chapter Two

Methodology

Since its emergence as a scholarly discipline, whiteness studies has been criticized for its lack of scientific rigor. In 2001, American historian Eric Arnesen published a journal article in Cambridge University's *International Labor and Working Class History* titled "Whiteness and the Historians' Imagination," where he insisted that weakness in methodology made whiteness studies practically worthless, as did arbitrary and inconsistent definitions, and a lack of grounding in archival and other empirical evidence.[1]

In 2009, according to "An Empirical Assessment of Whiteness Theory: Hidden from How Many?," researchers found that one of the most frequent and important criticisms of whiteness studies "involves the empirical grounding upon which the claims of whiteness scholars are based," and that "these critiques have involved questions about both the interpretation of key events and documents as well as the type and amount of empirical evidence that supports these analyses." The researchers go on to state in their paper:

> With only a few exceptions (e.g., Bush 2004; Helms 1990), empirical work on whiteness in the United States has been historical, case based, and qualitative. The lack of attention to measurement and the empirical generalizability of core claims and assumptions has actually been a source of frustration to some of the strongest proponents of whiteness scholarship within the social sciences. Ashley Doane, for example, writes that one "major shortcoming of much of the existing literature on whiteness is its lack of empirical grounding" (Doane and Bonilla-Silva 2003:17). Monica McDermott and Frank Samson point out that the lack of measurement has important theoretical implications: "[A]ttempts at specifying concrete ways in which the process of white racial identity formation varies or experiences of whiteness differ have been considerably lacking ... Consequently, we have no standard way of classifying how whiteness, or any other dominant group identity, is experienced" (2005: 256).[2]

In 2020, the discipline still suffers from some of the same flaws, as whiteness scholars tend to discredit the scientific method as biased—favoring qualitative anecdotal observations over quantitative data—and often insist that Western epistemology is nothing more than domination by Eurocentric white men.[3] Jonathan Church, a writer and government economist, is one of America's most outspoken critics of the methodologies of whiteness studies in general and white fragility theory in particular, and has published his work in numerous magazines such as *Quillette*, *The Agonist*, *Areo*, *Merion West*, and the *Good Men Project*. In an article titled "Whiteness Studies: An Insidious Ideology," he writes:

> Meanwhile, Whiteness scholars show no interest in exploring conceptual ambiguities and empirical shortcomings that might emerge from any rigorous unpacking of intricate ideas like individualism, objectivity, identity, color-blindness, and white privilege. Concerns about whether the core tenets of Whiteness Studies are conceptually sound, empirically verifiable, or falsifiable are therefore dismissed as exhibitions of white fragility. The upshot is a handy fragility trap arising from a conceited presumption of infallibility. Armed with this disingenuous method, DiAngelo and the rest can dismiss any objections to their core tenets—or indeed to any other aspects of Whiteness Studies—on the assumption that such objections are invalid because they are made by a "defensive" white person helplessly steeped in the invisible ideology and discourse of whiteness.[4]

Church goes on to write that because of such flaws, "Whiteness Studies must be resisted, because it leaves us in the dark of Plato's cave, without the tools of reason and evidence to make our way out into the light. Only indoctrination, and its twin sister intolerance for dissent, are permitted."[5]

OVERUSE OF IMPLICIT BIAS

Twenty-first-century America is becoming increasingly tolerant and racially diverse. Barack Obama won two terms as president, despite the fact that in 1960, nearly two-thirds of Americans said they'd never vote for a black man.[6] Likewise, acceptance of interracial marriage—which is often viewed by sociologists as the ultimate stage of assimilation of minority groups into society—has increased exponentially, up from just 4 percent in 1958 to 87 percent in 2004; amazingly, black–white marriages were still illegal in sixteen states until 1967.[7] In short, overt racism in America is dying, as most people do not harbor the same blatant prejudiced and discriminatory attitudes as did their grandparents.

But according to antiracists working within the field of whiteness studies, racism has not subsided—it's simply changed forms. A concept known as "new racism" has emerged, which teaches that racism has adapted over time so that white supremacy can still exist in society, producing the same inequality of the past while not appearing to be explicitly racist.

Under the blanket term "new racism" falls the idea of "colorblind racism"—when well-meaning whites perpetuate inequality by supposedly acting as if race has no impact; "aversive racism"—when well-meaning whites perpetuate inequality by refusing to acknowledge their own complicity in systemic racism; and "cultural racism"—when society supposedly begins instilling in children as young as preschool, via media, film, and a white supremacist educational system, that whites are superior to people of color.[8]

The common denominator of all these forms of "new racism" is the absence of overt, individual acts of prejudice and discrimination. In other words, whites who are guilty of new racism do not exhibit any hateful or intolerant behavior, and do not feel as though they are bad people or are doing anything wrong. As DiAngelo has documented in her workshops, most whites who practice new racism will insist that they are open-minded and care about social justice and the fight for racial equality. So how is it that these well-meaning whites are complicit in perpetuating racism and white supremacy on a daily basis?

The answer lies in something called implicit bias—the hidden prejudice that lies below a person's awareness and is outside of conscious control. According to DiAngelo, most people are wrong to assume that they control their own behavior because humans only have conscious access to a small fraction of their brains' emotional and cognitive process—about 2 percent to be exact. The other 98 percent of our brain works without our conscious awareness, and it's this part that is dictating the majority of human behavior. Because of this, DiAngelo insists implicit biases are pervasive and widespread.[9]

Indeed, the concept of implicit bias is at the heart of both whiteness studies and antiracism, and is the theoretical glue that holds these frameworks in place. Without implicit bias, the notions of colorblind racism, aversive racism, cultural racism, white supremacy, white privilege, white fragility, and a dozen other new and emerging concepts coined by scholar-activists like DiAngelo, would collapse like a house of cards.

Incredibly, as noted previously, the science behind implicit bias is questionable, a large portion of it stemming from twenty years' worth of results from the Implicit Association Test (IAT), which has since been shown to exhibit problems with both validity and reliability. Even the designers of the test admit that the results are less than perfect, placing a disclaimer on their website which states that the researchers and schools associated with the tests "make no claim for the validity of these suggested interpretations."[10]

As *New York Magazine* writer Jesse Singal states:

A pile of scholarly work, some of it published in top psychology journals and most of it ignored by the media, suggests that the IAT falls far short of the quality-control standards normally expected of psychological instruments. The IAT, this research suggests, is a noisy, unreliable measure that correlates far too weakly with any real-world outcomes to be used to predict individuals' behavior—even the test's creators have now admitted as much. The history of the test suggests it was released to the public and excitedly publicized long before it had been fully validated in the rigorous, careful way normally demanded by the field of psychology. In fact, there's a case to be made that Harvard shouldn't be administering the test in its current form, in light of its shortcomings and its potential to mislead people about their own biases.[11]

Problems stemming from the IAT aside, the concept of implicit bias has other issues. As with the negative connotations associated with "white supremacy," the term "implicit bias" has accusatory undertones which tend to imply a moral judgment against the person for whom the term is being applied. Ironically, research shows that implicit bias trainings often make things worse—closing minds and provoking resentment among participants instead of bringing receptiveness and unity.[12]

As with much of antiracist education, there's a certain provocative element built into the concept of implicit bias, a mechanism designed to call whites out so they can no longer filter race from the reality of their lives; indoctrinating whites to believe that they have an unknown amount of unconscious racial discrimination lurking in their brains effectively develops white racial identity, and helps them further embrace antiracist ideology.

In March 2018, a Philadelphia high school hosted a training on implicit bias sponsored by the Philadelphia School District's Office of Student Rights and Responsibilities.[13] The facilitator, a young African American woman, proceeded to show the faculty staff national statistics on school discipline, and how black males were three times as likely to be suspended or expelled as their white counterparts. The facilitator explained this was the result of implicit racial bias, and that teachers needed to look closely at their own beliefs in order to unpack their unconscious discriminatory attitudes.

Although some of the younger teachers listened attentively, there was immediate pushback from the older members of the faculty. Both white and black teachers alike—many of whom had dedicated their lives to educating, coaching, and mentoring their students—protested that they were indeed fair and open-minded, that their classroom management was based on positive behavior supports and sensitive to the cultural diversity of their students. And on the rare occasion that they formally pink-slipped a child and requested a suspension, it was always for high-level behavior infractions, such as fighting, or an assault on another student or faculty member.

The young facilitator pressed on with her implicit bias training nonetheless, repeating the statistics on the disparity between the discipline outcomes of whites and blacks, at times pausing to tell the staff that it was okay, they were still good teachers, but they just needed to unpack the racist ideas lurking in their psyches. The evidence of these biases, she said, was sitting right there in Harvard's IAT test. The fact that none of the teachers in the room had ever taken the IAT test didn't matter, nor did the fact that the IAT test had already been debunked as unreliable.

The figurative temperature of the room went up ten degrees, as many faculty members were frustrated at the implication that they were somehow unconsciously prejudiced. How could this be? They cared for their students like their own children, and had a very special connection with many of them.

At lunchtime, the teachers went off with their circles of friends, venting about what had just taken place. One faculty member got into a discussion with a colleague, and passionately pointed out how the statistics presented in the PowerPoint analyzed white teacher populations only, and that no other demographic was represented. Were whites the only ones who had implicit biases? Were teachers of color free from harboring prejudices? Either way, the workshop was demoralizing to many of the staff.

"It's not a good idea to go around telling teachers they are bigots," another teacher said. "Not with all the things we do in here, with the little resources we have." It was true. The workshop didn't help matters. In fact, it was deflating and quite counterproductive.

The major takeaway from the workshop ended up being this point, which the school's principal very astutely made: when it comes to teaching and disciplining very diverse student populations, it's better to be proactive rather than reactive. It was a valid point. Teachers shouldn't act impulsively or be quick to react. This was indeed something all educators as human beings—regardless of race or ethnicity—could learn to do better.

So why didn't the facilitator simply state this from the beginning, without dressing it up in the divisive, demoralizing language of race? *Be proactive rather than reactive.* So simple and clear. But unfortunately, the presentation wasn't simply about fair discipline and effective instruction, it was also about forwarding the politics of race, too.

This is a common theme in American education today. In July 2018, Texas high school English teacher Melissa Garcia wrote an article for *Education Week* headlined, "Why Teachers Must Fight Their Own Implicit Biases," explaining the importance of first impressions at the beginning of a new school year:

> In these moments, as students mingle and shyly interact with one another, we the teachers begin to make the very crucial observations that will affect our perceptions, and thus inform our expectations, of each student that school year. Research has shown that before teachers even have a conversation with a

student, they have already formulated a number of opinions based on that student's race, appearance, and other factors—and begun to form a certain set of expectations.[14]

In a nutshell, she cautions teachers not to judge a book by its cover when dealing with new pupils, which is good advice; teachers should be proactive instead of reactive, and remain fully present with their students by staying in the moment without labeling or judging them. Only Garcia doesn't use the words *don't judge a book by its cover*, or *be proactive rather than reactive*, or *be fully present without labeling or judging*. She chooses the phrase *implicit bias*, the preferred term of antiracists and whiteness scholars who tend to place the dualistic politics of race over the science of education.

This is concerning when it comes to the American classroom, as identity politics can be divisive and extremely polarizing, impacting the attitude and objectivity of educators trying to present instruction in an equitable manner. To measure how the concept of implicit bias is influencing learning, more research must be done to measure its actual influence and outcomes.

THE DUBIOUS NATURE OF MICROAGGRESSIONS

A side-effect of the supposed pervasiveness of implicit bias is a microaggression—the ongoing slights and insults people of color endure on a daily basis at the hands of well-meaning but racially illiterate whites. Harvard psychiatrist Chester M. Pierce first coined the term in 1970, but it wasn't until 2007, when Derald Wing Sue and six colleagues in the Teachers College at Columbia University published their paper "Racial Microaggressions in Everyday Life," that the concept took hold in mainstream America.

The paper defines microaggressions as "brief and commonplace daily verbal, behavioral, or environmental indignities, whether intentional or unintentional, that communicate hostile, derogatory, or negative racial slights and insults toward people of color." Those who commit microaggressions "are often unaware that they engage in such communications when they interact with racial/ethnic minorities."[15]

The professors created a taxonomy of microaggressions "through a review of the social psychological literature on aversive racism, from formulations regarding the manifestation and impact of everyday racism, and from reading numerous personal narratives of counselors (both White and those of color) on their racial/cultural awakening."[16]

Thus it was determined that microaggressions have three forms: a "microassault," which is an explicit verbal or nonverbal attack meant to hurt a person of color; a "microinsult," which is a subtle rude or insensitive communication that demeans a person of color's heritage or identity; and a "microinvalidation," a communication that excludes, negates, or nullifies a person of color's feelings, thoughts, or experience. The professors ultimately concluded that "nearly all interracial encounters are prone to the manifestation of racial microaggressions."[17]

Not surprisingly, there was pushback from researchers who disagreed with the findings. In a journal article called "Macrononsense in Multiculturalism," University of Wisconsin professor Kenneth R. Thomas called the paper "interesting but critically flawed," arguing that microaggressions are not unique to interracial interactions, and that everyone, regardless of race, experiences such messy indignities throughout the course of everyday life.[18]

University of Florida professor Rafael S. Harris Jr. also questioned the concept in an article titled "Racial Microaggression? How Do You Know?," suggesting that a microaggression committed against Derald Wing Sue and his African American colleague on an airplane may have been misinterpreted.[19] And East Tennessee State University College of Medicine professor Thomas E. Schacht pointed out that "micro" interactions may occur in any domain of interpersonal process, not merely the negative domains emphasized by Sue and his colleagues.[20]

Sue et al. responded to these criticisms in a journal article explaining that microaggressions are indeed race-based, and that the critics of his paper were unable to see the racial implications being that they were privileged white males. Sue and his colleagues also reasoned that because people of color are often treated like criminals by society—a reality not experienced by whites—racial minorities were in a better position to see and experience the harmful effects of microaggressions, and as a result, their experiential realities should be validated and accepted over the perspectives of privileged whites.

Ironically, Sue et al.'s objection to society's criminalization of people of color did not stop them from using criminalizing language in a 2019 paper aimed at stopping unconscious bigotry titled "Disarming Racial Microaggressions: Microintervention Strategies for Targets, White Allies, and Bystanders," where whites were labeled "perpetrators" who must be "disarmed," and where racial minorities were "targets" who needed to engage the help of "bystanders" who bore witness to the crimes.[21]

The divisive nature of such language was another example of the hypocrisy of antiracism in that it didn't aim to simply remedy racial injustice, but to also inflict a kind of retribution against those who were viewed as "racist," even if they were only unconsciously so. One would assume a true social justice advocate would call for the abolishment of all judgmental and derogatory language, not simply the transference of such language from one group to another.

As Schacht pointed out in his criticism of microaggressions:

> In contrast to this seemingly one-sided construction, a psychotherapeutic analysis of dysfunctional interpersonal patterns generally benefits from considera-

tion from the contributions of all actors. Each member of a therapeutic dyad acts and reacts, remembers and constructs, projects and internalizes, in a complex, cyclical, and recursive interpersonal and psychodynamic dance that defies simple reductive description or ascription of responsibility to one actor. In applying this perspective to the phenomena addressed by Sue et al., it may be helpful to remember that whenever two people engage in an unconsciously hostile interpersonal dance, neither party is merely a perpetrator, and arguably, in meaningful ways both are victims.[22]

In other words, it takes two to tango, and *both* parties—whites as well as people of color—must learn to communicate better, and be more aware of their interpersonal interactions. But as is so common with antiracism, only whites are at fault and must change their behavior. Still, despite such double standards, the concept of microaggressions continues to gain steam, and scores of colleges and universities are now offering workshops for faculty members on how to identify and avoid engaging in such subtle behaviors.

In September 2019, the School District of Philadelphia offered such a training titled "Equity vs. Equality," where high school teachers across the city were required to complete a half-day workshop that was designed using many of the antiracist elements espoused by DiAngelo.[23] Part of the purpose was to make educators more aware of their personal identities in order to allow them to unpack their implicit biases and disarm their microaggressions, which in turn would help them provide a more equitable education to all students.

One particular section of the training was facilitated by a thirty-something African American woman, who to her credit, was extremely friendly and welcoming. But her warm presence did little to soften the provocative and dualistic nature of the curriculum, which from the outset of the training, caused a small stir in the room.

Each teacher was provided a small packet of exercises to complete. The first exercise was a "Personal Identity Wheel," which required participants to choose their identity from a list of seven categories: "queer," "white," "gender conforming bio female," "middle class," "educated," "Christian," and "able-bodied." Next to each category was a brief description summarizing the identity. The "white" identity was defined as follows: "I am very privileged due to my white identity and have done a lot of personal work around my white privilege, so this is an area that I am more conscious of now than I was only 5 years ago."[24]

The wording immediately struck one of the white teachers as strange. Specifically, the belief that he was "very privileged" due to his whiteness was off-putting because it was making a sweeping generalization. In addition, the notion that he had "done a lot of personal work around my white privilege" was quite pretentious in its assumption that he had even subscribed to the concept of white privilege in the first place.

This was yet another example of how identity politics were not based in science, but in *politics*. And what made the designer of this curriculum think all teachers shared their politics? Antiracism isn't about debate, it's about indoctrination; to those activists pushing the implementation of this curriculum, the ultimate acceptance of white privilege by all teachers was a foregone conclusion.

The definition of "Gender Conforming Bio Female" was as follows: "I am targeted due to the fact that I am female, and women are still oppressed in our society. However, I am also privileged because my sex (genitals/genes) match my gender identity, which for some is not true. I am pretty aware of being a woman/female on a daily basis due to interacting with a lot of men."[25] Depending on the categories selected, each teacher was told that they were either "privileged and advantaged," or "targeted and oppressed," apparently to give them an understanding of how their students felt in the classroom and society, and to help them appreciate the value of diversity.

The reactions of the white teachers—who made up about 60 percent of the participants—matched pretty closely with what DiAngelo has described in her books. Some remained silent and personally withdrew from the training, quietly smoldering in their seats. Others agreed and offered polite support. One white male teacher chose to strike a balance, conceding some of the points while challenging others. He respectfully raised his hand and explained that he felt the categories were stereotypes—overgeneralizations of complex issues and people.

The facilitator remained politely neutral. She then transitioned into the fact that systemic racism, which targets people based on race and identity, was responsible for a wide array of racial injustices in America. She changed the PowerPoint slide to show statistics highlighting the racial disparities in housing, healthcare, net income, and educational attainment in America. "This is all based on one thing," she said, holding up a finger. "And that's racism."

After the training was over and the white male teacher returned to school the following day, a colleague of his—who happens to be biracial—asked him what he thought about the workshop. The white teacher told his biracial colleague he felt it was too political, and didn't really have any practical purpose other than promoting identity politics. The biracial teacher agreed, and admitted to the white teacher that he had ruffled a few feathers in his own section of the workshop, which was being held in a separate classroom down the hall.

In particular, the biracial teacher said he voiced an objection to the term "targeted," explaining that this created an element of intentional malice that didn't need to exist among people, and felt it would lead his students to believe that they were being victimized by society. The word "disadvantaged" would be more appropriate, he suggested. The facilitator leading the workshop refused to concede the point, and after a brief argument, the teacher was told he was "biased" and needed to unpack his unconscious resistance; the facilitator making the assessment was neither a counselor nor a psychotherapist of any kind.

Several weeks later, a district-wide survey was given to teachers evaluating the training, and the results showed that 45 percent of respondents said that there was not enough time provided to plan how their learning would be integrated into their practice, and 35 percent said they were not leaving with a "next step" they could implement in their classroom.[26] There was no "next step" because the purpose of the workshop wasn't rooted in instructional strategy; rather, identity politics.

Despite this lack of instructional planning and the development of a practical purpose for classroom implementation, advocates of whiteness studies would most likely deem the workshop a success, as the majority of Philadelphia high school teachers were further indoctrinated with the tenants of anti-racism, and were further convinced of their own implicit biases and microaggressions; how this made these men and women better teachers was still unclear by the end of the workshop.

EPISTEMOLOGICAL PROBLEMS

As evidenced by the theoretical shortcomings of implicit bias and microaggressions, whiteness studies is plagued by a lack of scientific rigor, and has numerous flaws. In DiAngelo's case, her work lacks sufficient statistical analysis, and is supported primarily by anecdotal observations and qualitative data, which don't allow her to formulate her claims as testable, falsifiable hypotheses. In an article titled "The Epistemological Problem of White Fragility Theory," published in December 2018, Jonathan Church analyzed DiAngelo's methodology. Church wrote:

> In short, statistics provides a framework for data analysis that allows a scientist to go beyond the realm of personal intuition derived from qualitative distillations of anecdotal observations. This is of utmost importance when studying the prevalence of racism and fragility in the entire white population of the United States. Regardless, without statistics, DiAngelo claims to have observed consistent, frequent and general patterns in her work. She draws on these patterns to develop a litany of examples, which allegedly demonstrate the *racialized* experience of white people, its relevance to racial inequality, and how it instills, influences and sustains the implicit biases that underlie white complacency about the institutional construct of racism (i.e., white supremacy)....
>
> [T]he theory of white fragility, and its practical application in DiAngelo's work, are couched entirely in terms amenable to its confirmation rather than its falsifiability. This is reflected most starkly in the discovery that there is not

one example in her research of rigorous hypothesis testing using statistical techniques. Her claims are based exclusively on qualitative assessments of her observations of white people interacting with people of color in group settings. Objections are invariably explained away as manifestations of white fragility. . . .

In failing to make use of statistics, DiAngelo's theory of white fragility is presented as non-falsifiable. As such, it cannot be distinguished from pseudoscience. DiAngelo offers us no way of evaluating whether she commits a type 1 or type 2 error when she makes one of her innumerable assertions about how the reactions of white people, when confronted with their alleged racialization and privilege, exhibit white fragility.[27]

As Church rightly observes, the bulk of whiteness studies—especially the work of DiAngelo—is presented with theories that don't allow for rigorous hypothesis testing, and are structured in ways that are biased toward confirmation rather than falsification. As Church states, "[I]t is hard to take seriously any research that consistently and frequently makes comprehensive claims about patterns in social life, without ever once having made competent use of hypothesis testing to conduct an analysis of data empirically relevant to a claim about patterns in social life."[28]

In short, the methods employed by whiteness scholars in general, and by DiAngelo in particular, still lack the kind of scientific rigor necessary to make the discipline epistemologically sound.

RECOMMENDATIONS

1. The scientific method is not based on race, but on objective universal rational inquiry that transcends ethnicity. As such, a more science-based approach is needed in whiteness studies as a whole, one that also includes quantitative data to test hypotheses, and abides by the principle of falsification.

2. America's students, teachers, and educational communities should not be subjected to microaggression workshops that criminalize its participants. Whites should not be labeled "perpetrators" who must be "disarmed," and racial minorities should not be viewed as "targets" who need the help of "bystanders" to bear witness to a crime. Such language is counterproductive and divisive, and does nothing to open people's minds, let alone bring racial harmony or understanding.

3. Microaggressions and implicit bias are dubious in nature, and based on flawed science. Whiteness scholars must either strengthen the science behind these concepts, or find alternative supports for their work. While some level of unconscious bias may exist between the races, both whites and people of color must learn to better communicate with each other equally, as a shared responsibility is the only path to mutual understanding.

NOTES

1. Eric Arnesen, "Whiteness and the Historians' Imagination," *International Labor and Working-Class History*, No. 60 (Fall, 2001), pp. 3–32.
2. Douglas Hartmann, Joseph Gerteis, and Paul R. Croll, "An Empirical Assessment of Whiteness Theory: Hidden from How Many?," Society for the Study of Social Problems, Vol. 56, No. 3 (August 2009), pp. 403–424.
3. Jack Niemonen, "Antiracist Education," *The American Sociologist*, Vol. 38, No. 2 (June 2007), p. 161.
4. Jonathan Church, "Whiteness Studies: An Insidious Ideology," *The Agonist*, July 1, 2019, http://theagonist.org (accessed January 1, 2020).
5. Ibid.
6. Larry Elder, "The Meaning of Charleston," *Townhall*, June 25, 2015, https://townhall.com (accessed January 11, 2020.)
7. Jack Ludwig, "Acceptance of Interracial Marriage at Record High," *Gallup*, June 1, 2004, https://www.gallup.com (accessed January 11, 2020).
8. Robin DiAngelo, *What Does It Mean to Be White?: Developing White Cultural Literacy Revised* (New York: Peter Lang, 2016), 124–135.
9. Ibid., 59–60.
10. "Preliminary Information," *Project Implicit*, https://implicit.harvard.edu/implicit/takeatest.html (accessed January 11, 2020).
11. Jesse Singal, "Psychology's Favorite Tool for Measuring Racism Isn't Up to the Job," *The Cut*, January 11, 2017, https://www.thecut.com (Accessed January 11, 2020).
12. Frank Dobbin and Alexandra Kalev, "Why Diversity Programs Fail," *Harvard Business Review*, July–August, 2016, https://hbr.org (accessed November 30, 2019).
13. Christopher Paslay, "Diversity Training Shouldn't Be Based on Flawed Implicit Bias Research," *Philadelphia Inquirer*, June 14, 2019, https://www.inquirer.com (accessed January 20, 2020).
14. Melissa Garcia, "Why Teachers Must Fight Their Own Implicit Biases," *Education Week*, July 25, 2018, https://www.edweek.org (accessed January 11, 2020).
15. Derald Wing Sue, Christina M. Capodilupo, Gina C. Torino, Jennifer M. Bucceri, Aisha M. B. Holder, Kevin L. Nadal, and Marta Esquilin, "Racial Microaggressions in Everyday Life," *American Psychologist*, Vol. 62, No. 4 (2007), pp. 271–286.
16. Ibid.
17. Ibid.
18. Kenneth R. Thomas, "Macrononsense in Multiculturalism," *American Psychologist*, Vol. 63, No. 4 (2008), pp. 274–275.
19. Rafael S. Harris Jr., "Racial Microaggression? How Do You Know?" *American Psychologist*, Vol. 63, No. 4 (2008), pp. 275–276.
20. Thomas E. Schacht, "A Broader View of Racial Microaggression in Psychotherapy," *American Psychologist*, Vol. 63, No. 4 (2008), p. 273.
21. Derald Wing Sue, Sarah Alsaidi, Michael N. Awad, Elizabeth Glaeser, Cassandra Z. Calle, and Narolyn Mendez, "Disarming Racial Microaggressions: Microintervention Strategies for Targets, White Allies, and Bystanders," *American Psychologist*, Vol. 74, No. 1 (2019), pp. 128–142.
22. Thomas E. Schacht, "A Broader View of Racial Microaggression in Psychotherapy," *American Psychologist*, Vol. 63, No. 4 (2008), p. 273.
23. "9/27 Equity vs. Equality," Office of Teaching and Learning, Student Rights and Responsibilities, The School District of Philadelphia, September 27, 2019.
24. Ibid.
25. Ibid.
26. "PD Survey: September 27, 2019," Office of Research and Evaluation, the School District of Philadelphia, October 2019.
27. Jonathan Church, "The Epistemological Problem of White Fragility Theory," *Areo*, December 18, 2018, https://areomagazine.com (accessed January 5, 2020).
28. Ibid.

Chapter Three

Anti-Bias Training

On March 12, 2020, Malvern Preparatory School, an elite Catholic academy located in Malvern, Pennsylvania, hosted a diversity conference led by Robin DiAngelo. The Head of School, Fr. Donald F. Reilly, emailed a letter to parents informing them of the workshop, explaining that diversity was a top priority of the school's board of trustees and leadership team, and that DiAngelo's book, *White Fragility*, was being read and discussed by the board, faculty, and staff in preparation for her lecture. The letter also informed parents that academic classes would be cancelled the day after the conference, on March 13, to allow Malvern's staff to regroup in meetings to unpack what they heard and experienced.[1]

The conference was done in partnership with the Association of Delaware Valley Independent Schools (ADVIS), and registration was open to the surrounding community. The following objectives for the talk were listed on the ADVIS website:

- Provide a shared framework for differentiating between: prejudice, discrimination, and systematic racism
- Understand the basic dynamics of current race relations in the U.S.
- Examine the concept of whiteness and white racial socialization
- Identify and make everyday patterns of whiteness recognizable
- Recognize common barriers to bridging racial divides and introduce the skills necessary for bridging them
- Recognize the above as an ongoing process and build motivation to continue
- Identify resources for supporting the work of racial equity[2]

The conference was switched to a webinar and done via the internet because of the growing panic over the coronavirus. The virtual program began at 9:00 a.m., with Robin DiAngelo speaking from her home in Seattle, Washington. Ali Michael, Director of the Race Institute for K–12 Educators, and Toni Graves Williamson, Director of Equity and Inclusion at Friends Select School in Philadelphia, were co-presenters. DiAngelo ironically opened by telling everyone she had no magic bullet to end racism, and that she wasn't going to give any specific methods or strategies for doing so. She suggested we listen with an open mind, however, and that the most important thing to do—especially for white people—was to engage in self-reflection.

The presentation proceeded with DiAngelo going through the same points covered in her books *White Fragility* and *What Does It Mean To Be White?* She explained how white people had no understanding of the realities of people of color, and expressed no interest in understanding these realities. She detailed how whiteness was hostile and oblivious, and how keeping white culture in place required ignorance. Her goal was to break up white solidarity, to expose whiteness, and to help white people "to be a little less white," which meant "to be a little less racially oppressive, to be a little less ignorant, and to be a little less arrogant."[3] She reiterated the idea that the status quo of white society was racism.

She insisted that all whites were racially illiterate and ignorant about race, because they hadn't undergone a sustained study, focus, and struggle on the topic. Textbook knowledge and a lifelong commitment to the politics of antiracist ideology was the only path to true enlightenment, and cross-racial relationships, biracial family interactions, and daily experience in diverse racial settings were discounted and considered false credentials. Whites could only have valid opinions with advanced degrees in whiteness studies and antiracism, thus making whiteness scholars the only people with opinions that were considered valid and informed.

And while whites could have no understanding of the reality of people of color, and could never truly comprehend the dynamics of race and racism at play in society, people of color were the experts on such matters without any academic knowledge, because their lives were filled with white oppression, and the reality of race was inescapable for them.

DiAngelo lectured on the topic of systemic racism, and how it was beyond the control of any one person, because it was infused across all institutions and existed at all levels of society. When DiAngelo began speaking of "anti-blackness" (a topic that will be addressed in chapter 9), a white high school teacher who was in attendance asked DiAngelo a question via the Q&A dialogue box, which was posted on the screen for all the participants to see. The question was: "Is anti-whiteness needed to stop anti-blackness?" This question was the only one in the Q&A box at the time.

DiAngelo ignored it, lecturing about the impact of growing up white—and how white people must grapple with the question of how race shapes their lives. America was a white supremacist society, and in order for people of color to achieve equality and gain proper access to resources, whites would have to unpack their privilege and end their white dominance and oppression. It was then that the white high school teacher asked his second question: "If it's up to whites to yield power to people of color, and people of color can't empower themselves independent of whites, isn't this perpetuating white supremacy?"

DiAngelo finished her talk promptly at 11:00. It was time for the designated thirty minutes of Q&A, and there were only three questions in the Q&A box, two of which were from the white high school teacher. These two questions were ignored, while the third question was addressed. There was a pause when DiAngelo finished her answer. The white teacher's questions sat there. Ali Michael, the white female presenter from the Race Institute for K–12 Educators, chimed in on the issue at hand, which pertained to white privilege.

The topic shifted to white fragility in the classroom, and so the same white high school teacher asked his third question: "Do you suggest telling students that they suffer from white fragility if they question antiracist viewpoints?" No response. For the remainder of the Q&A, every single question that came up in the Q&A box was addressed but those from the white teacher.

At 11:30, DiAngelo finished and signed off, but not before making a final statement. She concluded by saying that she understood that most of the white people participating in the conference would probably go home and do nothing, that they would forget the lecture and continue to lead their lives, refusing to become active in antiracism. She had a parting message for those people: to go home and look in the mirror, and to say to yourself, "I choose to collude with white supremacy."[4]

Ali Michael and Toni Graves Williamson began their talk about affinity groups in schools. Michael is the author of several books, one of which is titled, *Raising Race Questions: Whiteness, Inquiry and Education*, which won the 2017 Society of Professors of Education Outstanding Book Award. A guiding principle in the book states, "A multicultural curriculum is not sufficient for building an antiracist classroom."[5]

Michael went first, detailing her experiences with antiracist learning spaces and affinity groups, which were basically educational groups that focused on the politics of decentering whiteness and promoting the identities of marginalized groups. She said that affinity group conversation should be nonjudgmental, yet proceeded to say that all-white spaces were not good, outside of antiracist learning spaces.

At which point the same white high school teacher asked: "You say we shouldn't be judgmental, but state that all-white spaces 'are not good.' Isn't this judging?" No response. Michael proceeded to show slides about white fragility, and explained that "No White Fragility" zones shouldn't be about intolerance, but about growth and understanding. The white teacher asked another question: "Why must whites who have a different perspective be called names and labeled 'fragile,' etc.?" No response.

Michael turned her attention to a slide which showed two teenage girls—one white, one black—holding a sign that said *Pro Black Isn't Anti White*, and went on to explain how young people can be pro-black and stand for antiracism without being anti-white, and that those two concepts didn't counteract each other. So the white teacher asked the following question: "Isn't calling all whites 'racist' anti-white?" No answer.

But of course antiracism *was* anti-white, and everyone attending the webinar—including Michael herself—knew this was true. As DiAngelo had taught that very morning, whiteness was oppressive, hostile, arrogant, and racist by default. Antiracism was clearly anti-white and zero-sum, in that it required whites to acknowledge their privilege so they could willfully decenter or dismantle it in order for people of color to gain advancement. All-white spaces were "not good," and were an example of the kind of oppressive white supremacy culture that needed to be exposed and dismantled.

What *wasn't* anti-white was the more unifying approach of multiculturalism, which celebrated diversity and promoted inclusion through unity and a more universal value system. Unfortunately, though, multiculturalism was considered too tame by most antiracists, including Michael herself.

But that was the trick of the antiracist: to convince the world antiracism wasn't anti-white. It was irony at its finest. In the foreword to DiAngelo's *White Fragility*, Georgetown sociology professor Michael Eric Dyson wrote that whiteness "is a category of identity that is most useful when its very existence is denied. That's its twisted genius."[6] So antiracists were doing the very thing they railed against: hiding their identity. There was indeed a "good/bad" binary of racism, only it existed at a systemic level, not an individual one. At a societal level, whiteness equaled racism and oppression, thus whiteness was bad. Conversely, antiracism exposed and dismantled oppressive whiteness, thus it was good.

As all antiracists including DiAngelo preached, you were either racist or antiracist, there was no neutral. You either remained silent and colluded with white supremacy, or got politically active and fought for equality. It was zero-sum: all or none. The gain of one group was predicated on the loss of the other.

Michael and Graves Williamson decided, at 12:15, that they wouldn't start fielding questions yet, because they said there were fewer questions than normal. They continued talking about affinity groups. The white high school teacher's questions sat in the Q&A dialogue box, in plain sight of all the participants. They were summarily ignored. At 12:20, two questions came in from other participants about the racial makeup of antiracist learning spaces. Both questions were addressed, taking up the remainder of the time.

All told, there were seventeen questions asked by participants during the entire workshop, all of which were still sitting in the Q&A box: six from the white high school teacher, and eleven from other participants. None of the white teacher's six questions were acknowledged, and all eleven of the other questions were thoughtfully answered.

The session ended. Curious as to how members of the Malvern Prep school community felt about DiAngelo's lecture, the white high school teacher contacted the parents of a white Malvern Prep student by telephone, and asked them several questions (these interviews were conducted in confidentiality, and the names of the interviewees are being withheld by mutual agreement). The teacher wanted to know if they knew of Robin DiAngelo, and what they thought about her white fragility theory.

Were they aware of the ideology she was espousing? Did they believe that all whites were racist by default, and that white silence was perpetuating a white supremacy culture? Were they worried that Malvern Prep teachers—who were given DiAngelo's workshop—would bring such things into their child's classroom? In short, were they ready for a culture of antiracism, white privilege, and white fragility?

The white high school teacher spoke to the father first. In the spirit of full disclosure, this man was a friend of the teacher's, as they were from the same neighborhood as kids. The father told the teacher he'd heard of Robin DiAngelo, and that he did not agree with her perspective of the world. In particular, he felt her message about racism and white privilege was a slap in the face. "Does she know how hard I work?" he said. "Does she know how much I've sacrificed to send my son to a school like Malvern?"

When the white high school teacher explained to him the antiracist definition of "white privilege," he still felt frustrated, insisting DiAngelo was an out-of-touch ivory tower academic, who never had any real world experiences in a diverse, working class culture. The teacher informed him that DiAngelo grew up poor in an all-white community, but this didn't change his opinion. He argued she was still trying to indoctrinate the Malvern staff, and his son by default, with her radical and outrageous whiteness ideology, which stemmed from what he called a "mental illness."

"People like her make people like me racist," he said, stating that her constant blaming and scapegoating of white people was making him angry and resentful. He said she was part of the problem when it came to race relations in America, and that her excuse-making wasn't helping anyone, especially people of color. He said he believed anyone, no matter their race, could achieve if they worked hard and made the right decisions. He said he taught his son to work hard and respect people, no matter their race or background.[7]

The mother was very similar to her husband. She was annoyed by Malvern's decision to bring in DiAngelo, because there were both teachers and students of color in the school, and the school community was already welcoming and open to diversity. She felt DiAngelo, and her antiracist approaches which blamed and scapegoated whites, were not solving any problems, but making things worse.

She said she worked hard her whole life and earned what she had, and felt the concept of "white privilege" was insulting, and didn't apply to her family. More importantly, she said her son and his friends were irked at being called "privileged," and felt resentful toward the school that the administration would bring in a speaker like DiAngelo. "Not all of Malvern's students are spoiled rich kids," she said, echoing her son's frustration.[8]

These responses were telling, in that they fit the profile described by both DiAngelo and whiteness scholars in general. But they also fit the pattern described in the studies on diversity training, research that showed such trainings can actually make things *worse*. How many other Malvern parents and students felt resentment toward DiAngelo and her confrontational antiracist approach was unclear, but an empirical study on the effects of whiteness studies—and how these approaches are impacting morale in America's schools—is long overdue.

MANDATORY VS. VOLUNTARY TRAINING

Lee Jussim, a social psychologist, professor, and longtime writer who recently doubted the validity of stereotype threat on Twitter and subsequently triggered a Harvard graduate student (see chapter 8), believes mandatory implicit bias training is a bad idea.[9] The world of implicit bias, Jussim notes, is rife with issues: it remains controversial in scientific circles, because it's not even clear what most implicit bias methods actually measure. Likewise, its ability to predict discrimination is questionable, as is its overall reliability. Interestingly, implicit bias trainings seem to be gaining popularity, especially in the world of education and corporate America. This is concerning, as Jussim writes in *Psychology Today*:

> My view is that this is wildly premature—and potentially even dangerous. The overselling of implicit bias has, in my view, along with several other wildly oversold concepts (microaggressions, stereotype threat, white privilege), contributed to the toxic environment on many campuses and in some corporations in which speech is considered "violence," and in which, if you say the wrong thing, you can be denounced, ostracized, and even fired. And by "wrong thing," I am not talking physical threats or sexual harassment. I am talking

about making intellectual arguments against affirmative action, acknowledging the evidence that biology contributes to some demographic group differences, or even simply showing a debate regarding Canadian speech laws.[10]

In 2017, Jussim had an exchange with Dr. Mahzarin Banaji, one of the most prominent psychological scientists working in the area of implicit biases, who, along with Dr. Tony Greenwald and Brian Nosek, created the concept of implicit bias. Dr. Banaji, although an advocate of responsible implicit bias training, admitted that "[p]sychology and sociology data suggest that mandatory training is not as good as voluntary training. Mandatory training has the potential for backlash."[11]

A 2016 study published in the *Harvard Business Review*, which analyzed 30 years of diversity training data from more than 800 U.S. companies, showed that on the whole, such programs not only fail, but can even *decrease* diversity.[12] As stated in the Harvard article, force-feeding such training on people "can activate bias rather than stamp it out."[13]

Curiously, when it comes to antiracist educators working within the field of whiteness studies, such information falls on deaf ears. The reality that decades of diversity and anti-bias training is at best inconsequential, and at worst, creating more problems—matters little to those invested in identity politics. For folks like DiAngelo, antiracist ideology must be implemented at all costs, hence the creation of white fragility theory.

And how is this making teachers, parents, and principals feel after attending trainings where they are being told they are "fragile," "biased," "privileged," or are silenced or even reprimanded for simply daring to question the facilitator's ideological script? The recent debacle in New York City schools over its racially charged anti-bias trainings presents an interesting answer to this question.

NEW YORK'S TOXIC RACIAL ENVIRONMENT

In May of 2019, New York City Schools Chancellor Richard Carranza held a school administration seminar aimed at rooting out "white-supremacy culture" in the city's Department of Education (DOE).[14] The training contained a slide presentation with a bullet-point list of fourteen hallmarks of such culture, which included "individualism," "defensiveness," "power hoarding," and "objectivity." The list was based on the book *Dismantling Racism: A Workbook for Social Change Groups*, by Kenneth Jones and Tema Okun, and was part of a mandatory training given to principals and central office supervisors.

There was also a "White Privilege Exercise," where administrators had to reflect on their own racial identities. According to a story in the *New York Post*:

> The DOE did not immediately respond to a request for comment about the materials used for the administrators' training, but one adviser said that if the program's frankness is making people uncomfortable, that's because it's working.
>
> "It requires discomfort," said Matt Gonzales, who serves as an outside adviser on the DOE's school diversity task force and is a director of New York Appleseed, an advocacy group for school integration.
>
> "Having to talk about someone's own whiteness is a requirement for them to become liberated."
>
> Several recent attendees of the DOE's overarching implicit-bias training sessions—mandatory for all, including teachers—have bristled at the program's emphasis on the inherent insidiousness of "white" culture.
>
> White employees who object when accused of harboring deep-seated bias are branded "fragile" and "defensive," one insider who received the training has said.[15]

Whether or not the program was working was unclear, but one thing was certain: it was provoking resentment and bitterness among school district staff. Carranza's use of anti-bias training to dismantle "white supremacy culture" in schools sparked a major backlash, prompting administrators, teachers, and parents to call parts of the workshops "ugly and divisive." Specifically, teachers were told by diversity consultants to "focus on black children over white ones," and one Jewish superintendent who described her family's Holocaust tragedies "was scolded and humiliated."[16]

One such anti-bias training also included showing parents a racial-advantage hierarchy with whites at the top and blacks at the bottom, and with Asian students conveniently absent. A parent of an Asian child asked about the omission, and was told by consultants that Asians were near the top, "in proximity to white privilege," and were benefiting from "white supremacy," which outraged some parents and Asian activists.[17]

"The entire effort is a toxic brew of grievance and ignorance," wrote *New York Post* opinion columnist Michael Goodwin. "Instead of educating children, Carranza is indoctrinating them to believe they are society's victims."[18] In an article headlined, "Quit the racial demagoguery and start working for better schools," *New York Post* writer Karol Markowicz blamed Carranza's race-baiting for an offensive comment made by Jackie Cody, a member of a city schools advisory board. Apparently, Cody had referred to Asians as "yellow folks" in a group email. Markowicz also blamed Mayor Bill de Blasio for standing idly by, writing:

> Carranza and de Blasio have set the tone of the conversation about schools. People who agree with their race-obsessed proposals are "us," and anyone who disagrees is "them." And the thems must be minimized and destroyed as racists or idle rich people who don't care about kids.

Lucas Liu, a member of Community Education Council 3, said about Cody's comments: "I think this is representative of the environment Carranza has created. It's a toxic racial environment pitting parents against each other." Precisely.[19]

Three high-level DOE administrative executives who had been demoted or stripped of duties under Carranza's sweeping changes sued the DOE for $90 million, claiming he had created "an environment which is hostile toward whites."[20] The veteran administrators, all white women, claimed they'd been pushed aside for less qualified persons of color, and that there was a toxic whiteness concept going on.

"The bottom line is that he's making hiring decisions based on race and gender, and that's unlawful," said Davida Perry of Schwartz Perry & Heller. "That's a distortion of the New York City Human Rights Law." Perry also added, "You can't correct discrimination with adding more discrimination."[21]

Several months later, in September of 2019, a fourth women sued New York City's DOE. According to the *New York Post*:

> A former city schools administrator filed a $20 million discrimination suit against the Department of Education and Chancellor Richard Carranza on Monday, claiming she was relentlessly demeaned and forced from her job for being white.
> Leslie Chislett became the fourth plaintiff to accuse Carranza of creating an atmosphere in which white DOE employees are "swiftly and irrevocably silenced, sidelined and punished" if they object to being stereotyped by their minority colleagues.
> Chislett's Manhattan Supreme Court suit says her treatment included a May meeting where co-workers stood up in succession to bash her for being incapable of "doing the work" of racial equity.[22]

Chislett's lawsuit, according to the *New York Post*, claimed "the DOE has been plunged into a state of racially fixated dysfunction where whites who object have been cast as irredeemable racists incapable of leadership and deserving of belittlement."[23] Ironically, Chislett had just successfully spearheaded the DOE's AP for All program, an initiative praised by de Blasio as one of his administration's signature education accomplishments because of its racial inclusiveness. Nonetheless, DiAngelo's white fragility theory seemed to come into play here, as Chislett's objections were dismissed as either ignorance or defensiveness.

During a June 2018 presentation titled "Beyond Diversity," senior DOE executive Ruby Ababio-Fernandez explained that "there is white toxicity in the air and we all breathe it in" and that the goal of her lecture was to "interrogate whiteness." Chislett objected, and was "marked as not willing to do the work of diversity."[24]

Chislett's lawsuit stated that on June 27, 2018, Carranza told assembled staffers at DOE headquarters to "get on board with this equity platform or leave," and that this statement, according to the suit, was a "totalitarian threat to his employees' salaries and financial future that Carranza used to silence Caucasian DOE employees impact by his discriminatory actions for no other reason than their race."[25]

When Chislett clashed with an underling named Deonca Renee about her attendance at a meeting she was supposed to run, Renee told Chislett "how dare you approach me out of your white privilege." At this point, Renee began publicly attacking Chislett at meetings, and questioned her commitment to the cause. During a meeting in May, Chislett was singled out by Ababio-Fernandez as a dangerous dissident who should leave. "Sitting among us there are those that don't believe," Ababio-Fernandez told a room of fifty people, at which point Chislett was supposedly castigated in ritual fashion.[26] According to the *New York Post*:

> Ababio-Fernandez "permitted other members of [the Office of Equity and Access] to stand up in protest of Chislett, one-by-one stating names of children in their life that motivated them to pursue equity work and that they were protecting from people like Chislett," the suit states.
>
> During the same meeting, "numerous members of the team were permitted to literally stand and berate Chislett, in her workplace, and openly shame her by saying 'You are not willing to do the work,' despite her contributions to AP for All's accomplishment of its goals."[27]

Again, such behavior is the hallmark of the implementation of white fragility theory, in that the feelings and comfort of whites are sacrificed for the supposed greater cause of racial equality. As with much of antiracist education, the double standard between whites and people of color is glaring.

While the feelings and experiences of African Americans and Latinos are protected with the highest of care—as evidenced by the fight not only against overt racism but also against invisible transgressions such as implicit biases and microaggressions—the same courtesy is not extended to whites, who are basically told to "get over it" when they are triggered or offended. And if they can't get over it, they will be driven out or summarily removed, like Chislett and the other white New York City DOE executives who sued the city.

But the double standard at the core of white fragility is only part of the problem. Even more concerning is what such things are doing to America's teachers, administrators, parents, and schools.

RECOMMENDATIONS

1. Mandatory implicit bias training is a bad idea. The world of implicit bias remains controversial in scientific circles, and it's not even clear what most implicit bias methods measure. Likewise, its ability to predict discrimination is questionable, as is its overall reliability. Anti-bias training should remain voluntary to those who want to participate.

2. An empirical study on the effects of whiteness studies—and how these approaches are impacting morale in America's schools—is much needed and long overdue.

NOTES

1. Fr. Donald Reilly, email letter to Malvern Prep parents/guardians and students, February 29, 2020.
2. "MCRC@ADVIS Critical Conversations," ADVIS, March 12, 2020, https://www.advis.org/default.aspx?relID=756017595 (accessed March 16, 2020).
3. Robin DiAngelo, Ali Michael, and Toni Graves Williamson, "ADVIS Critical Conversations: White Fragility and Affinity Group Webinar," Association of Delaware Valley Independent Schools, March 12, 2020.
4. Ibid.
5. Ali Michael, *Raising Race Questions: Whiteness, Inquiry and Education* (New York: Teachers College Press, 2015), 4.
6. Robin DiAngelo, *White Fragility: Why It's So Hard for White People to Talk about Racism* (Boston: Beacon Press, 2018), iii.
7. Telephone interview with father of Malvern Prep student, March 12, 2020.
8. Telephone interview with mother of Malvern Prep student, March 12, 2020.
9. Lee Jussim, "Mandatory Implicit Bias Training Is a Bad Idea," *Psychology Today*, December 2, 2017, https://www.psychologytoday.com, (accessed March 1, 2020).
10. Ibid.
11. Ibid.
12. Frank Dobbin and Alexandra Kalev, "Why Diversity Programs Fail," *Harvard Business Review*, July–August 2016, https://hbr.org (accessed March 1, 2020).
13. Ibid.
14. Susan Edelman, Selim Algar and Aaron Feis, "Richard Carranza Held 'White-Supremacy Culture' Training for School Admins," *New York Post*, May 20, 2019, https://nypost.com (accessed February 29, 2020).
15. Ibid.
16. Susan Edelman, "Teachers Allegedly Told to Favor Black Students in 'Racial Equity' Training," *New York Post*, May 25, 2019, https://nypost.com (accessed November 30, 2019).
17. Selim Algar, "DOE-Sponsored Group Said Asians Benefit from White Privilege: Parent," *New York Post*, May 26, 2019, https://nypost.com (accessed February 29, 2020).
18. Michael Goodwin, "Richard Carranza's Prejudicial Race Politics Have Gone Too Ffar," *New York Post*, May 28, 2019, https://nypost.com (accessed February 29, 2020).
19. Karol Markowicz, "Quit the Racial Demagoguery and Start Working for Better Schools," *New York Post*, November 24, 2019, https://nypost.com (accessed February 29, 2020).
20. Susan Edelman, "Schools Chancellor Richard Carranza Accused of Demoting Admins Because They Were White," *New York Post*, May 18, 2019, https://nypost.com (accessed February 29, 2020).
21. "Lawyer for Women Suing Dept. of Education Speaks Out," CBS New York, May 30, 2019, https://newyork.cbslocal.com (accessed February 29, 2020).

22. Susan Edelman and Selim Algar, "Fourth White DOE Executive Sues over Racial Discrimination," *New York Post*, October 1, 2019, https://nypost.com (accessed February 29, 2020).
23. Ibid.
24. Ibid.
25. Ibid.
26. Ibid.
27. Ibid.

Chapter Four

Culture Matters

Antiracist ideology is predicated on the belief that racism in society is pervasive, systemic, and all-encompassing, and is the *one and only* cause of inequality in America. Antiracist and National Book Award–winner Ibram X. Kendi argues that if we truly believe that all humans are equal, than disparity in condition can only be the result of systemic discrimination.[1] Coleman Hughes, an African American writer and columnist at *Quillette*—who famously spoke out against reparations for slavery at a Congressional hearing in June 2019—coined a term for such a belief: *the disparity fallacy*. Hughes writes:

> The disparity fallacy holds that unequal outcomes between two groups must be caused primarily by discrimination, whether overt or systemic. What's puzzling about believers in the disparity fallacy is not that they apply the belief too *broadly*, but that they apply it too *narrowly*. Any instance of whites outperforming blacks is adduced as evidence of discrimination. But when a disparity runs the other way—that is, blacks outperforming whites—discrimination is never invoked as a causal factor.[2]

Hughes offered some interesting examples to support his point. He cited a recent study on race and economic opportunity in the United States that showed when parental income was comparable, black women had higher college attendance rates than white men, and higher incomes than white women. Hughes also highlighted African American economist Thomas Sowell's observation that "as early as 1980, U.S. census data show black college-educated couples out-earning their white counterparts."[3] Facts like these, Hughes pointed out, are never presented as examples of discrimination in *favor* of blacks, and he was puzzled as to why the disparity fallacy only went in one direction.

Hughes also noted that inequality existed among many ethnic groups in America, but that these differences were rarely attributed to racism. He wrote:

> A cursory glance at the mean incomes of census-tracked ethnic groups shows Americans of Russian descent out-earning those of Swiss descent, who out-earn those of British descent, who out-earn those of Polish descent, who out-earn those of French descent in turn. If the disparity fallacy were true, then we ought to posit an elaborate system that is biased towards ethnic Russians, then the Swiss, followed by the Brits, the Poles and the French. Yet one never hears progressives make such claims. Moreover, one never hears progressives say, "French-Americans make 79 cents for every Russian-American dollar," although the facts could easily be framed that way. Similar disparities between blacks and whites are regularly presented in such invidious terms. Rather than defaulting to systemic bias to explain disparities, we should understand that, even in the absence of discrimination, groups still differ in innumerable ways that affect their respective outcomes.[4]

One way these groups differ, as Hughes acknowledges, is culture. From an antiracist perspective, believing culture plays a part in inequality is the epitome of racism. DiAngelo in particular has done much to explain away the reasons why traditionally Asian Americans haven't been handicapped by racist white supremacy culture (because they have skin that looks white, and because the term "Asian" is an incorrect generalization that doesn't accurately capture the various ethnicities and geographic regions within the group), and why African immigrants have been able to achieve success in America (they haven't faced the kind of generational oppression and hardships unique to American-born people of color).[5] But these explanations are limited and political in nature, and turn a blind eye to hard quantitative data that paints a broader picture.

Ironically, DiAngelo picks and chooses when it's okay to generalize and when it's not (you can label whites as racist, but not Asians as successful), and when society should see color (whiteness should be acknowledged in societal oppression, but blackness should be ignored in crime statistics). She even plays both sides of the fence when it comes to the concept of "race."

On one hand, she argues race doesn't technically exist biologically, which nullifies any argument connected to culture, but on the other hand, she insists it *does* exist as a social construct, which allows antiracists to lambaste white society as oppressive and institutionally racist.[6] But culture does matter, as do the values associated with it, especially when it comes to education. And pretending to be "culture-blind" for political reasons does a major disservice to the people DiAngelo and her clique of antiracists claim to support.

ASIAN AMERICANS

Antiracists struggle with the success of Asian Americans, and the fact that they've somehow managed to overcome several centuries of oppression and hardship. As mentioned previously, DiAngelo has helped develop an elaborate argument to explain that the term "Asian American" is incorrect, being that this category is comprised of cultures and ethnicities from a wide variety of geographic locations, and that "success" is relative, being that immigrating to America on a student visa is much different from arriving here as a refugee from an impoverished, war-torn nation.

In his book *A Different Mirror*, Berkeley professor Ronald Takaki also questions the idea that Asian Americans are the "model minority," further showing that the success of the Asian culture in the United States is indeed a dilemma for social justice advocates, as it weakens the notion that systemic racism and white supremacy are too powerful to overcome, and that the values of a group—what they prioritize and how they choose to live—can have a real impact on both the quality and manageability of everyday life.

But history speaks for itself. Asian Americans have faced discrimination and systemic oppression for hundreds of years. Although Takaki questions Asians as the model minority, he clearly documents their systemic oppression:

> Asian Americans began arriving in America long before many European immigrants. . . . As "strangers" coming from a "different shore," they were stereotyped as "heathen" and unassimilable. Wanted as sojourning laborers, the Chinese were not welcomed as settlers. During an economic depression, Congress passed the 1882 Chinese Exclusion Act—the first law that prohibited the entry of immigrants on the basis of nationality. The Chinese condemned this restriction as racist and tyrannical. "They call us 'Chink,'" complained a Chinese immigrant, cursing the "white demons." "They think we no good! America cut us off. No more come now, too bad!" The Japanese also painfully discovered that their accomplishments in America did not lead to acceptance. During World War II, the government interned a hundred twenty thousand Japanese Americans, two-thirds of them citizens by birth. "How could I as a sixth-month-old child born in this country," asked Congressman Robert Matsui years later, "be declared by my own Government to be an enemy alien?" In 1975, after the collapse of Saigon, tens of thousands of refugees fled to America from the tempest of the Vietnam War.[7]

Unfortunately, this kind of racial discrimination has continued into the twenty-first century. In December 2009, more than thirty Asian students were attacked "mostly by African American school mates" in South Philadelphia High School, an incident that finally brought national attention to the "severe and pervasive" racial harassment these students had been facing for years.[8]

Community leaders, such as Helen Gym of Asian Americans United, had complained about the harassment in the school since 2007, but the Philadelphia School District took little action; Superintendent Arlene Ackerman, who had downplayed the racial angle, had refused for more than a week to meet with the Asian students, who protested by staying out of school for eight days. This prompted the U.S. Department of Justice and the Pennsylvania Human Relations Commission to sue the Philadelphia School District, which ultimately settled a year later, agreeing to take action to stop the attacks and discrimination.[9]

Despite such hardships, Asians have still managed to excel in school. On standardized tests, Asians have the highest scores in nearly every subject from K–12, as evidenced by NCES's Early Childhood Longitudinal Study, and the results of the NAEP, ACT, and SAT. In graduate school, Asians score at or near the top in both the GRE and LSAT.[10]

In fact, Asians are so successful academically that Ivy League schools such as Harvard have been accused of capping their admissions. Even though in 2019, Asians made up 25.4 percent of Harvard's class of 1,950 students (quite remarkable being that Asians only made up 5.9 percent of the American population), a group called Students for Fair Admissions sued Harvard over what they claimed were unfair admission practices which supposedly discriminated against Asians.[11]

In terms of educational attainment, 89 percent of Asian Americans 25 years or older have a high school degree (second only to whites, who are at 93 percent), and 53 percent of Asians have their college degree (whites are a distant second, at 36 percent).[12] Financially speaking, Asians have the highest median household income of all races at $81,331 (2017 dollars), over $13,000 more than whites, who earn $68,145 annually.[13] Similarly, only 12 percent of Asians live in poverty, second only to whites at 10 percent; Asians are also second in homeownership at 57 percent, and have the lowest unemployment rate at 3.6 percent.[14]

A 2012 *New York Times* article titled "For Asians, School Tests Are Vital Steppingstones" gives an interesting insight into Asian culture when it comes to education. "It's all about hard work," said Riyan Iqbal, fifteen, referencing the grueling preparation it takes to get into New York City's top schools. The son of a taxi driver, Riyan said his parents motivated him with stories about the trials they endured back in Bangladesh, like walking to school with no shoes, fighting hunger pains, and having to endure floods and political unrest. "You try to make up for their hardships," Riyan said in the article.[15]

Ting Shi, a Chinese student interviewed in the piece, explained that his first two years in the United States were wretched. Incredibly, the article stated he "slept in a bunk bed in the same room with his grandparents and a cousin in Chinatown, while his parents lived on East 89th Street, near a laundromat where they endured 12-hour shifts. He saw them only on Sundays."[16] But Ting spent that time studying and attending classes after school and even in the summer, which eventually paid off: after passing the difficult entrance exam, he got accepted into the much sought-after Stuyvesant High School, where he could receive an accelerated education in math and science.[17]

Riyan and Ting were used to the pressure, as rigorous testing was common in their home countries. They were also used to their parents' "observance of ancient belief systems like Confucianism, a set of moral principles that emphasizes scholarship and reverence for elders, as well as their rejection of child-rearing philosophies more common in the United States that emphasize confidence and general well-being."[18] Which is another segment of culture Asians prioritize: marriage and family. In 2014, 68 percent of Asians twenty-five years and older were married, the highest of all racial groups in America. Likewise, only 13 percent of Asian children eighteen or younger lived with a single parent, the lowest in America.[19]

Ironically, Asians generally grow up in a colorblind household. According to DiAngelo, while "many African Americans relate to having been prepared by parents to live in a racist society . . . many Asian heritage people say that racism was never directly discussed in their homes."[20]

The values listed in the *New York Times* article—supported by the statistics from the U.S. Census Bureau and the Pew Research Center—also ring true in classrooms in Philadelphia. Teachers from a high school in the northeast section of the city have noted that their Asian students come from two-parent families that stress respect for authority, academic scholarship based in math, science, and the development of English language literacy, and have a healthy appreciation for academic competition; they also come from families that prioritize time management skills such as punctuality and meeting deadlines.

To attribute this success primarily to "colorism"—the fact that Asians "look white" and are therefore treated as white by society and placed higher in the racial hierarchy—is overly simplistic and tragically shortsighted.

WEST INDIAN AND AFRICAN IMMIGRANTS

Like Asians, West Indian and African immigrants have been able to achieve success in America, despite facing multiple hardships; nearly one-third of African immigrants come to the United States as refugees or asylees, fleeing extreme poverty, violence, oppression, and war in their home countries.[21] Tragically, once they get to America, they continue to face discrimination and other obstacles related to their foreign status. As Aminata Sy, founder and president of the African Community Learning Program, wrote for the *Philadelphia Inquirer* in 2019:

In the School District of Philadelphia, immigrants and native-born students of African backgrounds rarely see themselves reflected in curricula. What message does this absence of their people, their histories, their cultures send to children? "You don't belong—Philadelphia isn't your city, America isn't your country." Students of African immigrant backgrounds endure bullying for being African, "too black," or speaking English with an accent. Historically in America, Africans have been viewed through a stereotypical lens of wildlife and backwardness. These perceptions persist and continue to hurt Philadelphia children. A recent University of California study found that Africans are misrepresented and underrepresented in American media.[22]

Yet despite bullying, misrepresentations in the media, language barriers, and surviving extreme poverty and oppression in their homelands, a 2007 study by Princeton and University of Pennsylvania researchers found that black immigrants from the West Indies and Africa made up 41 percent of the black population of Ivy League schools, even though black immigrants only accounted for 13 percent of the black population of eighteen-to-nineteen-year-olds in the United States at the time.[23]

A 2015 Pew study showed that 35 percent of African immigrants twenty-five years and older had a college degree, an average 5 points *higher* than the general U.S. population. In addition, English language proficiency was higher among black immigrants (74 percent) than all other immigrant groups (50 percent), and although 20 percent of black immigrants lived below the poverty line—only 4 percent higher than the general U.S. population—this was 8 percent *lower* than U.S.-born blacks.[24]

As with Asians, black immigrants have a relatively strong family unit. The Pew study showed that 52 percent of African immigrants were married, and that 17 percent were divorced, numbers slightly stronger than the U.S. general population, which stood at 50 percent and 20 percent, respectively. Similarly, 53 percent of African immigrants lived in a married-couple household, which was 7 percent lower than the general population, but 17 percent higher than U.S.-born blacks.[25]

A 2018 Seton Hall dissertation by Sheila Newton Moses titled "Understanding the Academic Success of Black Caribbean Immigrant Students Who Have Earned a Graduate Degree at an Ivy League University" provides a further insight into the culture of successful black immigrants. The findings revealed that these students had strong individual intrinsic motivation, an abundance of parental and community support, took pride in cultural values that stressed hard work and the importance of school and education, and exhibited a positive mindset.[26] Moses wrote about the students she interviewed in her research:

> Some participants' families were working class and dedicated much of their efforts to making sure their children understood what was expected of them.

These families assured their children, that if they focused on academic excellence, they could eventually help their families financially. A strong work ethic was noticed by many of the participants' parents, and therefore this was reinforced in their psyche.[27]

As with research on Asian Americans, the Pew statistics and observations in the Moses doctoral dissertation matches the experiences of Philadelphia teachers. Educators from a high school in the northeast section of the city found their African students are highly motivated, organized, respectful, and come from strong, two-parent families. But unlike Asians, there is no "colorism" at play here; even DiAngelo won't argue that African immigrants "look white," and are thus treated as white by society and placed higher in the racial hierarchy. So what explains their success? They too, like American-born people of color, have faced generations of violence, disease, and oppression in their home countries. Perhaps cultural values have had some impact?

Interestingly, the majority of African Americans do not say discrimination is the main reason blacks on average have worse jobs, income, and housing than whites. According to a 2013 Gallup poll, 60 percent of blacks said these differences were caused by "something else."[28] The 2015 Pew study supported this. Besides racial discrimination, 75 percent said poor schools were a major reason why some blacks have had a harder time getting ahead, followed by lack of jobs (66 percent), family instability (57 percent), a lack of good role models (51 percent), and a lack of motivation to work hard (43 percent).[29]

Again, from an antiracist perspective, to suggest as much is treasonous and the ultimate form of blasphemy. To say the black race is responsible for their own circumstances in 2020 is hateful and racist. Ironically, it's not hateful and racist to say the *white race* is responsible for the circumstances of the black race, however, which is curious. Perhaps a better way to look at things would be to say that *both* races are responsible for racial outcomes in America, as both whites and blacks do have a certain level of control, if one wants to look at things honestly, and not from an antiracist perspective draped in identity politics.

Is white systemic racism a reason for racial disparities in the United States? Absolutely. But it's not the *only* reason. Cultural values are at least part of this complex equation, and antiracists like DiAngelo who refuse to acknowledge this reality must ask themselves the following question: *How will any group whose cultural values have zero impact on the outcomes of their own lives ever have any control over anything?* Just as DiAngelo says that colorblindness holds inequality in place by pretending not to see race in group disparities, so does culture-blindness hold inequality in place by pretending not to see how values impact the quality and manageability of life.

THE RACIALIZATION OF UNIVERSAL VALUES

For the politics of antiracism to work, the whole of society must be racialized. The goal isn't to judge people by the content of their character, *but by the color of their skin*. Which is why colorblindness is the new racism: because to choose to be colorblind, or to judge someone by a universal human value, is to undo the racialization of society, which hurts the antiracist's ability to use racism as a commodity and further the power of identity politics. From an antiracist perspective, inequality can never be attributed to values, as values are too closely related to culture.

But is limiting the complexities of inequality simply to racism the most productive way to bring about the positive change antiracists claim to seek? Are there indeed universal human values that transcend race and ethnicity that can be used by all people to succeed, values like family, work ethic, literacy, scholarship, time management, and respect for elders? One would logically think so, being that people of Asian, African, and West Indian decent have all used these values to improve the quality of their lives.

Yet antiracists seem to have a different perspective altogether. According to professors at the University of Maryland and the University of Iowa, expecting people of color to exercise such values is marginalizing their heritage and identity in an effort at white acculturalization. These researchers published a paper in the January 2019 issue of *American Psychologist* arguing that such values were not universal but based on white supremacist ideology. The researchers described "white culture" as follows:

> In the United States, *White culture* is described as a fixed constellation of Western values and beliefs that prioritize "rugged individualism, competition, action-orientation, hierarchical power structures, standard American English, linear and future time orientation, Judeo-Christianity, European history, Protestant work ethic, objective science, owning goods and property, the nuclear family unit, and European aesthetics."[30]

Yet people of various cultures have used most of these values to succeed. Asians, Africans, and those from the West Indies have all embraced competition, action-orientation, work ethic, scholarship, and the nuclear family unit. Asians in particular stress objective science, hierarchical power structures (a patriarchy that respects fathers and elders), and linear and future time orientation, and both Asians and Africans value learning standard American English. And not just in white Western society, but in their homelands and cultures.

It wasn't until the late 1970s and early 1980s, with the emergence of Critical Race Theory (CRT) and the mainstream popularization of Paulo Freire's 1968 *Pedagogy of the Oppressed*, that universal human concepts such as the family unit, linear time, objective science, work ethic, and respect for elders started to get readily dismantled and rebranded as "white." It was Freire who first suggested that the time-honored tradition of a teacher giving direct instruction to a student was a form of oppression, calling it the "banking concept of education" where knowledge was "a gift bestowed by those who consider themselves knowledgeable upon those whom they consider to know nothing."[31]

Instead, Freire taught a new concept known as "problem-posing education," where the banking concept was overcome:

> Indeed problem-posing education, which breaks with the vertical characteristic of banking education, can fulfill its function of freedom only if it can overcome the above contradiction. Through dialogue, the teacher-of-the-students and the students-of-the teacher cease to exist and a new term emerges: teacher-student with students-teachers. The teacher is no longer merely the-one-who-teaches, but one who is himself taught in dialogue with the students, who in turn while being taught also teach. They become jointly responsible for a process in which all grow. In this process, arguments based on "authority" are no longer valid; in order to function authority must be *on the side* of freedom, not *against* it. Here, no one teaches another, nor is anyone self-taught.[32]

Although this new "problem-posing" concept was groundbreaking in its articulation of how learning actually takes place (and in describing how the formation of knowledge is really a co-creation between teacher and student), it was used by antiracists to fundamentally transform not only instructional techniques by teachers but also to erode respect for "oppressive" authority; after Freire, school discipline was never the same.

For the past thirty-plus years, antiracists have piggy-backed off Freire's dualistic mantra of "oppressor vs. oppressed," and have sought to disrupt the institutionally racist American educational system further theorized in CRT. Incredibly, this has involved actively dismantling many of the universal values at the heart of American education by rebranding them as forms of "Western white racism."

For example, the scientific method has not only been reintroduced by whiteness scholars as racist epistemology practiced by Eurocentric white men—where subjective qualitative observations aimed at social justice often take precedent over objective quantitative data collection—but traditional math has been infused with identity politics at the elementary and high school levels.

In 2019, in an effort to push "culturally responsive pedagogy," the Seattle school district began promoting ethnocentric math via their "K-12 Math Ethnic Studies Framework," where learning objectives included asking questions like: *What is my mathematical identity? Who gets to say if an answer is right? How has math been used to resist and liberate people and commu-*

nities of color from oppression? When do I know/feel like I am a mathematician? Can you advocate against oppressive mathematical practices?[33]

The same approach is taking place in American ELA classrooms. Not only has Ebonics served to dismantle traditional grammar, but antiracists are now calling on English teachers to "disrupt texts" by dumping lesson plans based on universal themes in literature, and adopting activities that racialize classic novels and teach students to view such texts through the lens of racism and white oppression.

In a blog article on the International Literacy Association website titled, "Disrupting Your Texts: Why Simply Including Diverse Voices Is Not Enough," high school English teacher Tricia Ebarvia asks literature teachers to "resist colorblind readings of texts," to "consider the role that race and whiteness have played in your own socialization, particularly around your beliefs about schooling," and to "begin with the premise that public schools never intended to educate all children equally and look for the ways in which this holds true today," among other approaches.[34]

She states that "curriculum has never been neutral, but always ideological," and ironically, her remedy isn't to eliminate political ideology by focusing on concrete skills and universal themes that unify the races, but by injecting *more* political ideology into the lesson, ideology rooted in zero-sum identity politics.

Such approaches may be one reason why the international performance gap in education between the United States and the rest of the world is widening. The 2018 Programme for International Student Assessment (PISA) is a test administered every three years that measures what fifteen-year-old students have learned in math, reading, and science. According to *US News & World Report*, American researchers were troubled "that 30 countries scored higher than U.S. students in math and that the performance gap between top-performing and lower-performing students is widening, especially in reading."[35]

But antiracism doesn't stop with academics. Black Lives Matter has been pushing to dismantle the nuclear family, too. One of BLM's thirteen guiding principles, titled "Black Villages," states, "We are committed to disrupting the Western-prescribed nuclear family structure requirement by supporting each other as extended families and 'villages' that collectively care for one another, and especially 'our' children to the degree that mothers, parents, and children are comfortable."[36]

In January of 2017, a group of Philadelphia schoolteachers called the Caucus of Working Educators sponsored a "Week of Action" in city schools, asking that teachers across Philadelphia wear Black Lives Matter T-shirts and buttons, and use curriculum resources—based upon the thirteen Guiding Principles of BLM—to design lessons in their classrooms.[37] In July of 2018, the National Education Association agreed to adopt and promote a Black

Lives Matter "Week of Action" in schools during Black History month in 2019.[38]

Antiracists criticize the concept of linear time as institutionally oppressive as well. Brittney Cooper, associated professor of Women's and Gender Studies and Africana Studies at Rutgers, stated in a 2019 interview with NPR that "if time had race, it would be white," and that "white people own time."[39]

"So when I say time has a race, I'm saying that the way that we position ourselves in relationship to time comes out of histories of European and Western thought," she explained. "And a lot of the way that we talk about time really finds its roots in the Industrial Revolution. So prior to that, we would talk about time as merely passing the time."[40]

This is an argument antiracists have been making for years, that linear time is a white concept, and that educators must be cognizant of the fact that some of their students may not come from cultures that use Western time. Although one can argue that time has a cultural context to it (how tightly one culture abides by a set schedule can be subjective), but from an American educational standpoint, teachers should be more focused on instilling in their students the organizational skills needed to follow the time schedules put in place by society rather than on debating the validity of linear time itself.

At the root of this argument is the concept of cultural relativism—the idea that a person's beliefs and values should be understood based on that person's own culture and shouldn't be judged against the criteria of another—and that no one culture is better than another. However, the subjective argument of one culture being "better" than another is quite different from the more objective concept of a culture's manageability within the context of society. In other words, which cultural values allow the people of that culture to have the most access to resources and the best quality of life?

In some traditional African cultures, the concept of time is indeed more flexible and viewed as "a series of events," and a focus on tending to the immediacy of the present takes precedent over the future.[41] And while it might be valid to argue that tardiness is indeed a matter of cultural perspective, is it prudent to attribute the negative consequences of such tardiness solely to white supremacy while ignoring what the cultural value is doing to the manageability and quality of life of the "tardy" person within the context of Western society?

When it comes to practical things like FAFSA application deadlines, bell schedules, and college admissions interviews, it certainly isn't. A student with a relaxed concept of time who applies for FAFSA a week after the deadline will not be receiving any financial aid. Likewise, getting to class or a college admissions interview fifteen minutes late will lead to the frustration of low grades and college rejection letters. At which point the student may ask: *Why are these things happening to me?*

An antiracist would argue it's because of white supremacy culture, and that if America wasn't dominated by European white males and their obsession with linear time, things would be different. And in a philosophical way, this may be true. But in terms of the reality of everyday life in American society, railing against structural racism isn't going to bring this student any relief from his suffering. But helping him adjust his values—in particular, his time management skills—will undoubtedly increase his quality of life, and make his situation much more manageable.

RECOMMENDATIONS

1. Educators and whiteness studies scholars must resist the "disparity fallacy." Although systemic racism is a root cause of racial inequality, it's not the *only* cause, and refusing to acknowledge this fact is counterproductive and doing an extreme disservice to the educational system in America.

2. Culture matters, and has a real impact on education, as well as the quality and manageability of people's lives. Placing a value on family, scholarship, time management, work ethic, respect for elders, individual intrinsic motivation, and healthy academic competition is not "white supremacy culture," but a time-honored, universal approach used by numerous cultures across the globe to succeed and achieve. American educators should continue to stress these values, not dismantle them for political reasons, or promote an environment of "culture-blindness," which just perpetuates inequality by pretending that culture does not have an impact on life.

3. To improve math, science, and reading, American educators should center their lessons on the objective skills at the center of these subjects, not on activities rooted in identity politics. Social justice advocacy indeed has a place in schools, but the racialization of all subjects across all content areas is counterproductive, and as evidenced by America's low PISA scores, could be having a negative impact on the practical skills children need to succeed in college and beyond.

NOTES

1. Robin DiAngelo, *White Fragility* (Boston: Beacon Press, 2018), 26.
2. Coleman Hughes, "The Racism Treadmill," Quillette, May 14, 2018, https://quillette.com(accessed January 20, 2020).
3. Ibid.
4. Ibid.
5. Robin DiAngelo, *What Does It Mean to Be White?: Developing White Cultural Literacy Revised* (New York: Peter Lang, 2016), 299–326.
6. Ibid, 97–98.
7. Ronald Takaki, *A Different Mirror: A History of Multicultural America* (New York: Back Bay Books, 1993,) 7–8.

8. Dale Mezzacappa, "District Settles with Feds on South Philly HS," *Philadelphia Public School Notebook*, December 15, 2010, https://thenotebook.org (accessed January 23, 2020).

9. Ibid.

10. Christopher Paslay, "Ancient Chinese Secret: Why Asian Students Excel Academically," Chalk and Talk, December 16, 2012, https://chalkandtalk.wordpress.com (accessed January 23, 2020).

11. Charles Lam, "Harvard Announces High Admittance of Asian Americans as Judge Weighs Affirmative Action," NBC News, April 2, 2019, https://www.nbcnews.com (accessed January 22, 2020).

12. "On Views of Race and Inequality, Blacks and Whites Are Worlds Apart," Pew Research Center, June 27, 2016, https://www.pewsocialtrends.org (accessed January 23, 2020).

13. Kayla Fontenot, Jessica Semega, and Melissa Kollar, "Income and Poverty in the United States: 2017," United States Census Bureau, September 2018, https://www.census.gov (accessed January 23, 2020).

14. "On Views of Race and Inequality, Blacks and Whites Are Worlds Apart."

15. Kyle Spencer, "For Asians, School Tests Are Vital Steppingstones," *New York Times*, October 26, 2012, https://www.nytimes.com (accessed January 23, 2020).

16. Ibid.

17. Ibid.

18. Ibid.

19. "On Views of Race and Inequality, Blacks and Whites Are Worlds Apart."

20. Robin DiAngelo, *What Does It Mean to Be White?*, 17.

21. Monica Anderson, Mark Hugo Lopez, and Molly Rohal, "A Rising Share of the U.S. Black Population Is Foreign Born," Pew Research Center, April 9, 2015, https://www.pewsocialtrends.org (accessed January 24, 2020).

22. Aminata Sy, "Philadelphia's Many African Students Need Culturally Inclusive Education," *Philadelphia Inquirer*, February 19, 2019, https://www.inquirer.com (accessed January 24, 2020).

23. Evelyn Hsieh, "Following Obama, Students Define 'Black' on Ivy League Campuses," *Huff Post*, June 19, 2009, https://www.huffpost.com (accessed January 24, 2020).

24. "A Rising Share of the U.S. Black Population Is Foreign Born."

25. Ibid.

26. Sheila Newton Moses, "Understanding the Academic Success of Black Caribbean Immigrant Students Who Have Earned a Graduate Degree at an Ivy League University," Doctoral Dissertation, Seton Hall University, College of Education and Human Services, May 18, 2019, https://scholarship.shu.edu (accessed January 24, 2020).

27. Ibid., 80.

28. Frank Newport, "Fewer Blacks in U.S. See Bias in Jobs, Income, and Housing," *Gallup*, July 19, 2013, https://news.gallup.com (accessed January 25, 2020).

29. "On Views of Race and Inequality, Blacks and Whites Are Worlds Apart."

30. William Ming Liu, Rossina Zamora Liu, Younkyoung Loh Garrison, Ji Youn Cindy Kim, Laurence Chan, Yu C. S. Ho, and Chi W. Yeung, "Racial Trauma, Microaggressions, and Becoming Racially Innocuous: The Role of Acculturation and White Supremacist Ideology," *American Psychologist*, Vol. 74, No. 1 (2019), 143–155.

31. Paulo Freire, *Pedagogy of the Oppressed, 30th Anniversary edition* (New York: Continuum, 2000), 72.

32. Ibid., 80.

33. Madeline Fry, "In Seattle, Math Is Cultural Appropriation," *Washington Examiner*, October 23, 2019, https://www.washingtonexaminer.com (accessed January 25, 2020).

34. Tricia Ebarvia, "Disrupting Your Texts: Why Simply Including Diverse Voices Is Not Enough," International Literacy Association, September 5, 2019, https://www.literacyworldwide.org (accessed January 26, 2020).

35. Lauren Camera, "U.S. Students Show No Improvement in Math, Reading, Science on International Exam," *US News & World Report*, December 3, 2019, https://www.usnews.com (accessed January 25, 2020).

36. Christopher Paslay, "Commentary: Skip Black Lives Matter's Action Week in Philly schools," *Philadelphia Inquirer*, January 19, 2017, https://www.inquirer.com (accessed January 25, 2020).

37. Ibid.

38. New Business Item 4 (2018), National Education Association, 2018, https://ra.nea.org (accessed January 25, 2020).

39. "Brittney Cooper: How Has Time Been Stolen From People Of Color?," NPR, WSIU Radio, March 29, 2019, https://news.wsiu.org (accessed January 25, 2020).

40. Ibid.

41. John Parratt, "Time in Traditional African Thought," *Religion*, Vol. 7, No. 2 (1977), 117–126.

Chapter Five

Parents and Patriarchy

Jay Cooke Elementary School in Philadelphia had a problem with teacher turnover. Between 2012 and 2019, an alarming 131 teachers filled approximately thirty positions, and only a single teacher stayed all seven years. Twenty-five other Philadelphia schools faced a similar situation, most of which were located in the north and southwest sections of the city, neighborhoods comprised of the district's most vulnerable students.[1] Although discipline, school climate, and administrative support were identified as factors contributing to the teacher churn cycle, there was one underlying element that antiracists and educational advocates had mostly ignored: parents.

The stability of families impacts the stability of teachers. More than thirty years of research by the Educational Testing Service has established that children from stable, two-parent families have higher overall academic achievement, less behavioral and psychological issues, and less contact with police than children living in one-parent families.[2] The relationship between these factors and teacher turnover is obvious: educators are more likely to stay in schools where academic potential is high, and behavioral and psychological problems are low.

Advocating for family stability in education is not very popular, however. Schools are seen as the beacon of hope for communities, not the other way around. There's an unwritten law that reforming education should center on in-school factors that educators can control—such as the quality of teachers, principals, and the rigor of instruction. Putting attention on systemic problems such as the breakdown of the family isn't politically correct, and like acknowledging cultural within racial disparities, is considered by antiracists as blaming the victim.

Not *all* systemic issues are off the table when it comes to education reform, of course. Antiracists working within the fields of whiteness studies continue to lobby educators to end institutional racism in schools through the dismantling of white supremacy culture, microaggressions, and implicit racial bias, which unlike the focus on family, are very useful politically, and are considered social justice issues by antiracists; Teach for America, which has a history of political lobbying despite its nonprofit status, requires their Philadelphia recruits to explore their "assumptions and biases regarding race, power, and privilege" during their induction training.[3]

Which leads to the question: why *isn't* family stability a social justice issue? Don't Philadelphia children deserve a father just as much as they deserve ethnomathmatics or a classroom free from microaggressions? If getting rid of unconscious racial slights can increase math and literacy skills (which has yet to be adequately documented), imagine what advocating against father absence could achieve?

FATHER FACTS

According to statistics compiled by the National Fatherhood Initiative (NFI), children without fathers are more likely to face abuse and neglect; commit a crime and go to prison; abuse drugs and alcohol; and are twice as likely to drop out of high school. When it comes to girls, the father factor is even more important: daughters are less likely to engage in risky sexual behavior and become pregnant as teens when they have consistent contact and a feeling of closeness with their dads. Incredibly, children living in single-parent, female-headed homes have a poverty rate of 47.6 percent, four times the rate of two-parent families. In 2018, nearly 1 in 4 children lived in father-absent homes nationwide.[4]

Father absence is a problem that affects children across America. However, statistics from NFI's *Father Facts, Eighth Edition*, reveal that father absence impacts each culture differently. In 2018, 69.1 percent of all children under age eighteen in the United States lived with both parents, 22.2 percent lived with their mother only, 4.4 percent lived with their father only, and 4.3 percent lived with neither parent. The racial breakdown was as follows:

- Of all White children, 74.6% lived with both parents, 17.4% lived with their mother only, 4.4% lived with their father only, and 3.6% lived with neither parent.
- Of all Black children, 39.7% lived with both parents, 48.1% lived with their mother only, 5.03% lived with their father only, and 7.13% lived with neither parent.
- Of all Hispanic children, 67.0% lived with both parents, 24.9% lived with their mother only, 4.0% lived with their father only, and 4.2% lived with neither parent.

- Of all Asian children, 86.8% lived with both parents, 8.5% lived with their mother only, 2.2% lived with their father only, and 2.4% lived with neither parent.[5]

Consequences of father absence, as mentioned above, are concerning. Adolescents without fathers are at a significantly higher risk for substance and alcohol use, especially young men. Data from the 2012 National Survey on Drug Use and Health found that black males with nonresident fathers were significantly more likely to have smoked blunts (marijuana wrapped in tobacco leaves) in their lifetime than black males with resident fathers. In addition, a study with 441 college students showed that a poor relationship with one's father was highly related to depression, a common predictor of alcoholism for both females and males.[6]

Children without fathers are more susceptible to physical abuse and criminal activity. NFI's report found that "fathers were more likely to abuse their step-children, pointing to the increased risk of child abuse for children with absent biological fathers."[7] In 2013, an estimated 1,520 children died from abuse and neglect in the United States.

In terms of crime, researchers analyzed data on gun carrying and drug trafficking in young men, and linked father absence to the likelihood of engaging in these behaviors. They found that "father absence *was the only disadvantage* on the individual level with significant effects on gun carrying, drug trafficking, and co-occurring behavior," and that "individuals from father absent homes were 279% more likely to carry guns and deal drugs than peers who lived with their fathers."[8]

Most notably, using data from the National Longitudinal Study of Adolescent Health to explore the relationship between family structure and risk of violent acts in neighborhoods, NFI's report found that:

> A 1% increase in the proportion of single-parent families in a neighborhood was associated with a 3% increase in an adolescent's level of violence. In other words, adolescents who lived in neighborhoods with lower proportions of single-parent families and who reported higher levels of family integration committed less violence.[9]

Emotional and behavior problems are also linked to the absence of fathers. The NFI report found that having a father in the home was associated with a lower level of aggression in children. Researchers also found that "children whose fathers were absent at the time of their birth were at significantly greater risk of incurring various developmental diagnoses, as well as a significantly greater number of developmental diagnoses, such as attention/learning disorder and speech/language disorder."

In addition, financial support from a nonresident father was directly associated with children's cognitive development—findings that suggested a father's failure to pay child support "can lead to higher maternal economic hardship and stress, which can affect child development outcomes." Finally, researchers found that a biological father's consistent presence was positively associated with the ability of a toddler to regulate emotion.[10]

Father absence is also linked to low birth weight, higher infant mortality rates, and decreased cellular function. Children without fathers have a higher risk for obesity and injury, among other poor physical health outcomes. In terms of socioeconomics, children living in father-absent homes "are at greater risk for growing up in poverty, living in disordered neighborhoods, and experiencing food insecurity than are their peers in traditional family households."[11]

Still, from an antiracist perspective, such data is unimportant. *New York Times*–bestselling author Mychal Denzel Smith wrote an article for the *Washington Post*, titled "The Dangerous Myth of the 'Missing Black Father'," where he argued responsible fatherhood could only go so far in a world plagued by institutionalized oppression. Smith, who is black, started his article by stating, "Growing up, the lesson was everywhere: Every major problem in black America can be solved if we addressed the problem of missing fathers."[12]

He went on to reason that for black children, "the presence of fathers would not alter racist drug laws, prosecutorial protection of police officers who kill, mass school closures or the poisoning of their water," and insisted that by focusing on "the supposed absence of black fathers, we allow ourselves to pretend this oppression is not real, while also further scapegoating black men for America's societal ills."[13]

Smith's perspective on fatherhood is interesting. As is so common with the use of identity politics, facts and data are selectively applied. Smith cautions us not to focus on "the supposed absence of black fathers," as if black fathers weren't really absent, as if the entire fight to get missing black fathers to reengage with their children and families were just a "dangerous myth," as is stated in the headline of the article.

But it's not a myth, it's reality. Black fathers *are* missing, in fact, as 55 percent of black children live with either their mother only, or no parent at all. And pointing this out isn't to suggest "every major problem in black America can be solved if we addressed the problem of missing fathers," as Smith writes, but simply to show that a legitimate problem exists, one that must continue to be addressed, no matter how uncomfortable.

This is one of the fundamental flaws of antiracism in the field of whiteness studies: because it is zero-sum, it becomes an all-or-nothing proposition. Of course institutional racism exists, as do mass school closures, and lead-filled water. But *in addition to such things*, there is the importance of having a father, and ignoring or downplaying this fact does nothing to close the achievement gap or bring racial equality in America.

PARENTS AND EDUCATIONAL ATTAINMENT

The impact parents have on education is well documented. A 2009 report by the Educational Testing Service, titled, "The Family—America's Smallest School," highlighted that "children who live in single-mother families score lower on measures of academic achievement than those in two-parent families," and that the differences "are substantial (in statistical terms, about a third of a standard deviation after controlling for age, gender, and grade level)." The report also established a strong link between growing up in a single-mother family and having lower income as an adult.[14]

Child Trends, a nonprofit, nonpartisan research organization dedicated to improving the lives of children, issued a report titled, "Charting Parenthood: A Statistical Portrait of Fathers and Mothers in America," which stated:

> Studies report that children whose parents are involved in their schooling are more likely to earn high grades and enjoy school than children whose parents are not involved in their children's schooling. This result holds for students in both elementary and secondary school. Children of involved parents are also more likely to have higher educational aspirations and motivation to achieve. In addition, parent involvement in school is related to fewer student suspensions and expulsions and higher levels of student participation in extracurricular activities.[15]

One significant way parents can help their children academically is by reading to them. Research shows that reading to a child plays a big part in early language acquisition. According to Child Trends:

> Children develop literacy-related skills long before they are able to read. By reading aloud to their young children, parents can help them acquire the prerequisite skills they will need to learn to read in school. Being read to has been identified as a source of children's early literacy development, including knowledge of the alphabet, print, and characteristics of written language.
>
> By the age of two, children who are read to regularly display greater language comprehension, larger vocabularies and higher cognitive skills than their peers. Shared parent-child book reading during children's preschool years leads to higher reading achievement in elementary school, as well as greater enthusiasm for reading and learning. In addition, being read to aids in the socioemotional development of young children and gives them the skills to become independent readers and to transition from infancy to toddlerhood.[16]

Early childhood literacy development varies by race and socioeconomic status. In 2005, the Federal Interagency Forum on Child and Family Statistics measured the percentage of American children ages three to five who were read to every day in the past week by a family member. The results showed that 68 percent of whites read to their children every day, followed by 66 percent of Asian Americans, 50 percent of blacks, and 45 percent of Hispanics.[17]

The now-famous study by Betty Hart and Todd R. Risley, published in the book *Meaningful Differences in the Everyday Experience of Young American Children* in 1995, showed that the vocabulary of parents—coupled with the number of books available in the home—also impact child literacy development. Incredibly, by the age of four, children from professional families hear 20 million more words than children from working-class families, and 35 million more than children from families on welfare.[18]

In addition to aiding literacy development, parents can help children succeed in school by maintaining a stable address, and a home environment conducive to studying. "Parsing the Achievement Gap II," a 2009 report by the Educational Testing Service, showed that frequent school changing and television watching affected achievement in school, both of which varied by race. U.S. Census Bureau data revealed that black children changed schools much more frequently than white children, causing black students to fall below grade level in math and reading.

Similarly, black children watched nearly three times as much television as their white counterparts; research indicated that television watching took away from study time and school work, and had been shown to hurt SAT scores.[19]

The idea that family is important to the success and well-being of children is not new. In 1965, Daniel Patrick Moynihan, an Assistant Secretary of Labor, authored a report titled, "The Negro Family: A Case for National Action," which identified structural causes of the breakdown of the black family—discrimination, unemployment, and a flawed welfare system. Moynihan concluded that this was causing out-of-wedlock births among black children to increase, which meant that the number of black children living with their mothers only would continue to rise unless "national action" was taken.[20]

The report was controversial, and has been widely criticized by liberals for decades (Mychal Denzel Smith is one of these critics). Despite this, Moynihan's prediction came true. The number of black children under age eighteen who lived with one or no parent went from 33 percent in 1960, to 65 percent in 2005. Similarly, the gap between white and black male college graduates went from 12 percent in 1960, to 17 percent in 2005.[21]

Although antiracists insist such data is irrelevant—that institutional racism and white supremacy culture are the *only* reasons for the breakdown of black families and out-of-wedlock births—there are black scholars who believe otherwise. Henry Lewis Gates, an influential literary critic and the Alphonse Fletcher University Professor at Harvard University, stated:

> We do, however, know that the causes of poverty within the Black community are both structural and behavioral. Scholars as diverse as philosopher Cornel West and sociologist William Julius Wilson have pointed this out, and we are foolish to deny it. A household composed of a sixteen-year-old mother, a thirty-two-year-old grandmother, and a forty-eight year-old great grandmother cannot possibly be a site for hope and optimism. Our task, it seems to me, is to lobby for those social programs that have been demonstrated to make a difference for those motivated to seize these expanded opportunities.[22]

In 2009, a follow-up on the Moynihan Report was published. Titled *The Moynihan Report Revisited: Lessons and Reflections After Four Decades*, it was based on the papers and proceedings of prominent scholars who met at Harvard in 2007 to discuss the relevancy of the original report. The conclusion was clear: Moynihan got it right.[23] Despite all of this, antiracists working within the field of whiteness studies still shy away from acknowledging the power of the family, and refuse to make a child's right to a father a social justice issue.

TOXIC MASCULINITY AND PATRIARCHY

There's a reason why antiracists and social justice advocates invested in identity politics don't fight for a child's right to a father: because they are too busy fighting to end toxic masculinity and patriarchy. Today, men are rarely seen as mentors to their sons, or as protectors of their wives and daughters; in contemporary America, male behavior is viewed as something that needs to be corrected.

In 2019, the American Psychological Association issued its "Guidelines for Psychological Practice With Boys and Men," which stated that "traditional masculinity is psychologically harmful."[24] As with racism, white supremacy, and colorblindness, the concept of "masculinity" has been rebranded and given a more progressive definition to fit a social justice agenda based on identity politics.

Masculinity is not chivalrous, strong, courageous, or protective. It's not a man setting an example for his son by caring for his family and taking care of his responsibilities, or by teaching his daughter love and self-respect through his own attention to her needs. According to the APA, traditional masculinity is "marked by stoicism, competitiveness, dominance and aggression," and "is, on the whole, harmful." The APA goes on to say that men socialized in this way "are less likely to engage in healthy behaviors."[25]

In a 2005 study of mental health treatment in prison, the psychiatrist Terry Kupers defined toxic masculinity as "the constellation of socially regressive male traits that serve to foster domination, the devaluation of women, homophobia, and wanton violence."[26] The prevailing social-scientific understanding of masculinity, according to prominent Australian sociologist Raewyn Connell, is that masculinity is not fixed, but a product of relations and behaviors shaped by class, race, culture, and sexuality. Connell notes that "when the term *toxic masculinity* refers to the assertion of masculine privilege or men's power, it is making a worthwhile point. There are well-known gender patterns in violent and abusive behavior."[27]

In March 2018, University of Wisconsin education professor Kathleen Elliott published a paper titled, "Challenging toxic masculinity in schools and society," where she stated that a failure to adequately address toxic masculinity resulted in a culture that "continues to award power and status to men (particularly white men), despite how they behave or treat others," and that it was up to educators in schools to address the problem head-on.[28] DiAngelo refers to this problem as "patriarchy," which she defines as "a society in which men are seen as having the inherent right to rule over women."[29]

Traditionally, a "patriarch" is a male head of a family, just as a "matriarch" is a female head—both terms relatively benign in nature. However, as the feminist movement gained momentum in America, "patriarch" morphed into "patriarchy," and an innocuous word meant to describe the man of the house became a politicized term that suggested violence and oppression against women. As the *Guardian*'s chief culture writer Charlotte Higgins stated:

> The word literally means "rule of the father", from the ancient Greek. There are many different ideas about its extent and force. Some people have used it to describe patterns derived from the structure of the family; to others, it is an entire system of oppression built on misogyny and the exploitation and brutalisation of women. It is not simple, in fact, to produce a concise definition of patriarchy. But at its simplest, it conveys the existence of a societal structure of male supremacy that operates at the expense of women—rather in the way that "white supremacy" conveys the existence of a societal structure that operates at the expense of black people.[30]

When it comes to identity politics, the merging of things like race and gender is known as "intersectionality," a concept coined in 1989 by UCLA law professor and black feminist Kimberlé Crenshaw that explains how race, class, gender, and other individual identities "intersect" with one another.[31] Simply stated, antiracism isn't limited to race, as forms of oppression overlap among groups, and the fight for social justice for one marginalized group is in essence a fight for social justice for all marginalized groups.

But how is this focused fight against patriarchy and toxic masculinity impacting father absenteeism, and by extension, the education of youth in America? Chastising men for chauvinistic behavior can lead to positive change, granted, but when was the last time an entertainer, professional athlete, or other high profile father was publicly called out for shirking their duty as a dad? There are multiple stories of NFL players being suspended for accusations of domestic violence, but what about for walking out on their family?

As researchers state in NFI's *Father Facts, Eighth Edition*, "The duration of father absence is a factor in educational success, as is the quality of the father-child relationship. Family structure not only affects educational outcomes for children, but is also associated with educational expectations."[32]

Ironically, antiracists and social justice advocates ignore the most toxic male behavior of all: father absenteeism. In short, activists must start fighting for a child's right to a father, bad behavior or not. This would make a world of difference when it comes to America's schools.

RECOMMENDATIONS

1. Fathers matter, and have a significant impact on education, and the overall quality and manageability of life. Whiteness studies must do more to highlight the systemic absence of fathers across all cultures, and how this absence contributes to the disparity between racial groups in terms of the abuse and neglect of children; a young person's contact with police; the abuse of drugs and alcohol; risky sexual behavior; poverty; educational attainment; and income.

2. Family stability matters, and the breakdown of the nuclear family coincides with delayed language development and lower literacy rates, and correlates to an increase in behavioral problems in school. In addition to advocating against institutional racism, antiracist educators must call for a focus on the family, and the benefits of having two active parents in the household.

3. Whiteness studies must include an analysis of how fathers and the family impacts "privilege" and academic success in America, and the fight for social justice must be expanded to include a child's right to a father. Fighting against toxic masculinity and patriarchy has its place, but its overemphasis can become counterproductive in an educational setting.

NOTES

1. Jessica Calefati, Dylan Purcell, and Kristen A. Graham, "Turnstile Teaching," *Philadelphia Inquirer*, April 26, 2019, https://www.inquirer.com (accessed January 26, 2020).

2. Paul E. Barton and Richard J. Coley, *The Family: America's Smallest School* (Princeton, NJ: Educational Test Service, September, 2007), https://www.ets.org (accessed January 26, 2020).

3. Teach for America Greater Philadelphia, Certification & Training, https://www.teachforamerica.org (Accessed January 26, 2020).

4. National Fatherhood Initiative, *Father Facts 8*, 2019, https://www.fatherhood.org (accessed January 26, 2020).

5. Ibid, 7–8.

6. Ibid., 11–15.

7. Ibid., 14.

8. Ibid., 16–17.

9. Ibid., 18.

10. Ibid., 21–24.

11. Ibid., 26.

12. Mychal Denzel Smith, "The Dangerous Myth of the 'Missing Black Father'," *Washington Post*, January 10, 2017, https://www.washingtonpost.com (Accessed February 1, 2020).

13. Ibid.

14. Paul E. Barton and Richard J. Coley, *The Family: America's Smallest School*, 9.

15. Tamara Halle, "Charting Parenthood: A Statistical Portrait of Fathers and Mothers in America," Child Trends," 2002, https://www.childtrends.org (accessed January 29, 2020), 18.

16. Paul E. Barton and Richard J. Coley, *The Family: America's Smallest School*, 20.

17. Ibid., 21.

18. Betty Hart and Todd R. Risley, *Meaningful Differences in the Everyday Experience of Young American Children* (Baltimore, MD: Paul R. Brookes Publishing Co., 1995).

19. Paul E. Barton and Richard J. Coley, *Parsing the Achievement Gap II* (Princeton, NJ: Educational Test Service, April, 2009), https://www.ets.org (accessed January 29, 2020).

20. Paul E. Barton and Richard J. Coley, *The Black-White Achievement Gap: When Progress Stopped* (Princeton, NJ: Educational Test Service, July, 2010), https://www.ets.org (accessed January 29, 2020), 21.

21. Ibid, 21–23.

22. Ibid., 22.

23. Ibid., 23.

24. Stephanie Pappas, "APA Issues First-Ever Guidelines for Practice with Men and Boys," *American Psychological Association*, Vol. 50, No. 1 (2019), 34.

25. Ibid.

26. Terry A. Kupers, "Toxic Masculinity as a Barrier to Mental Health Treatment in Prison," *Journal of Clinical Psychology*, Vol. 61, No. 6 (2005), 714.

27. Michael Salter, "The Problem with a Fight Against Toxic Masculinity," *The Atlantic*, February 27, 2019, https://www.theatlantic.com (accessed January 31, 2020).

28. Kathleen Elliott, "Challenging Toxic Masculinity in Schools and Society," *On the Horizon*, Vol. 26, No. 1 (2018), 17–22.

29. Robin DiAngelo, *What Does It Mean to Be White?: Developing White Cultural Literacy Revised* (New York: Peter Lang, 2016), 63.

30. Charlotte Higgins, "The Age of Patriarchy: How an Unfashionable Idea Became a Rallying Cry for Feminism Today," *The Guardian*, June 22, 2018, https://www.theguardian.com (accessed January 31, 2020).

31. Kimberle Crenshaw, "Demarginalizing the Intersection of Race and Sex: A Black Feminist Critique of Antidiscrimination Doctrine, Feminist Theory and Antiracist Politics," *University of Chicago Legal Forum*, Vol. 1989, No. 1 (1989).

32. National Fatherhood Initiative, *Father Facts 8*, 18.

Chapter Six

Assault on Learning

Just as antiracists working within the field of whiteness studies have downplayed the importance of fathers and cultural values in education and society, they have also glossed over the reality of crime and violence in American schools and neighborhoods. In her book *What Does It Mean to Be White?*, DiAngelo includes an entire chapter on why whites should avoid using narratives that paint minorities in an unflattering light.[1] Titled "Stop Telling That Story! Danger Discourse and the White Racial Frame," the chapter argues that whites should refrain from speaking about situations that involve crime or violence and people of color.

"How we *think* and *speak* about people of color is a fundamental foundation for how we *treat* people of color," DiAngelo writes. "Discourse that specifically positions people of color as inherently dangerous, while simultaneously positioning whites as inherently innocent, has material consequences in the larger society."[2]

DiAngelo calls such conversation "danger discourse," which she claims comes from a "white racial frame," a concept that states whites use an internalized racist framework to make meaning of race, a framework built on images, perceptions, interpretations, and emotions based in white supremacy.[3] This discourse "distorts reality, trivializes the true direction of violence and positions whites as innocent."[4] It also reinforces white solidarity and maintains all-white spaces through segregation, DiAngelo insists, which allows whites to gain further social capital.

DiAngelo provides an example of danger discourse by referencing a comment her student made in a course called "Schools in Society," where a white girl, reflecting on her own racial frame, stated that her boyfriend had been "mugged by a black man." DiAngelo was troubled by the remark, being that the student mentioned race and didn't connect it to a broader point. Later in the semester, DiAngelo overheard a group of students in the hall apparently talking about their student-teaching placements.

"I grew up in a really sheltered neighborhood so I am scared to do my placement there," one student said, referring to Springfield, Massachusetts, a city that was 57 percent black and Latino at the time. Another student responded by saying, "Oh, I used to live in New Haven where I heard gunshots at the dance club, so Springfield doesn't scare me."[5]

DiAngelo cautioned against both statements in her book. In the first instance, the student described her suburban white neighborhood as "sheltered," which DiAngelo said was racially coded language for "innocence" and "safety," and which insinuated that non-white neighborhoods were not innocent or safe. The student also stated that she was scared to do her placement in Springfield, which according to DiAngelo, was an unfounded fear that stemmed from a white racial frame built on distorted racist images of black people being inherently dangerous.

The second student, who wasn't afraid of Springfield because she had heard gunshots at a dance club in New Haven, was also reinforcing the inherent belief that black neighborhoods were unsafe. But because she had not established any real relationships with inhabitants of these neighborhoods, she was not an expert on the subject, and had no contrary stories to tell that could humanize these residents by comparison.

Although the principle at the heart of DiAngelo's danger discourse is well-meaning, the concept suffers from a double standard. In particular, it conflicts with the antiracist notion of "colorblindness," which seems to change depending on the context of the situation. DiAngelo explains that "colorblind racism" is the ideology that pretending that we don't notice race will end racism, which is harmful because it denies racism and holds it in place.[6]

In effect, whites shouldn't deny that they see race, or that race matters, especially when it comes to the disparities in things like housing, healthcare, income, criminal justice, and education. In this context, seeing race is encouraged, because it is bearing witness to racial disparities, and as the saying goes, *sunlight is the best disinfectant.*

But as evidenced by DiAngelo's danger discourse, colorblindness is only discouraged in *some* situations—those that shield whites from criticism and accountability. When it comes to crime and violence in big urban cities and school districts, seeing race is frowned upon. In fact, in these situations, it is expected that whites *pretend that race doesn't exist*. In New York City in 2014, for example, blacks committed over three-quarters of all shootings, but only made up 23 percent of the city's population. Whites, on the other hand, committed less than 2 percent of all shootings, yet made up 34 percent of the city's population.[7]

To acknowledge this would be problematic, as seeing color in this context is considered danger discourse, and according to DiAngelo, serves no purpose other than to elevate whites and demean people of color.[8] Here, sunlight is *not* the best disinfectant, and ironically, it requires people to accept the ideology that pretending that we don't notice race in urban crime will somehow *end* this crime and make black neighborhoods safer, which of course, it will not.

Danger discourse implies a racial "us" and "them," DiAngelo teaches her students. Curiously, she doesn't appear too concerned that teaching her students to view the world through the dualistic lens of white oppressors/non-white oppressed, or privileged whites/disadvantaged blacks, will create a racial "us" and "them," however.[9]

The idea that danger discourse "distorts reality, trivializes the true direction of violence and positions whites as innocent" is also questionable, because it suggests that the discourse is false or exaggerated, when in fact it may not be. Urban areas like Springfield, Massachusetts, indeed have some sections that are dangerous and crime ridden, and a disproportionate amount of this crime is committed by people of color. In 2009, despite being only 15 percent of the population in the 75 largest counties in the United States, blacks were charged with 62 percent of all robberies, 57 percent of murders, and 45 percent of assaults.[10]

This isn't a distortion of reality, but a fact. Just like it was a fact that the boyfriend of the girl in DiAngelo's "Schools and Society" class was mugged by a black man, and that the girl discussing the student-teaching placement had heard gunshots at a dance club in New Haven. Further, suggesting that such realities are not the "true" direction of violence is a cause for concern, being that violence—no matter what the cause—is not acceptable, even if such violence stems in part from institutional racism.

Pretending not to notice race in urban crime will do nothing to end it. Nor will blaming these things on distortions caused by white racial framing. Like institutional racism, such problems need the disinfectant of sunlight, especially when these problems occur inside America's schools and impact children.

VIOLENCE AS A COPING MECHANISM

It's understandable that antiracist educators, in an effort to end negative stereotypes against people of color, would want to caution future teachers about using danger discourse. But the approach DiAngelo employs is disingenuous, and in the end is more about identity politics than it is about giving young people the skills and information needed to work in urban settings like Springfield, Massachusetts.

When a young person expresses concern about doing a student-teaching placement in an urban area, instead of chastising the person for using danger discourse—which in effect denies the existence of violence by blaming it on racism and distorted thinking—an appropriate response would be to acknowledge that the person's fear is valid, but that this anxiety may be overblown and based on a stereotype.

Here's where the use of generalizations becomes an issue for antiracists. The traditional approach for dealing with a student-teacher's fear of teaching in a big city would be to warn against stereotyping, and to explain that it's wrong to judge an entire group or region by a single standard. Sure, some parts of Springfield may have safety issues, and certain schools may be more challenging than others, but qualifying the whole of Springfield and its schools as "dangerous" is wrong, because there are many neighborhoods and schools that are safe and welcoming, and even the places that have higher crime rates are still home to lots of good, caring people.

But because overblown, sweeping generalizations are at the core of antiracism—such as the notion that all whites are systemically privileged and perpetuate racism by default, and that all people of color are systemically disadvantaged and are oppressed by default—an antiracist educator would be hard-pressed to preach against the use of overgeneralizing.

Still, instead of dwelling on the hypocritical nature of "danger discourse" (where seeing color changes depending on the political context of the situation), a professor intent on helping an anxious student-teacher might give some practical advice to a young person, advice meant to ease their fear and clear their mind of such stereotypical preconceptions. For example, a professor might suggest that the student-teacher learn ways to genuinely connect with their students and families, and that doing so will work wonders for their instruction and classroom management.

A professor might suggest that the student-teacher be truly authentic and not get caught up in the overly cerebral and often dualist concepts of identity politics—the view that society should be neatly categorized into oppressors/oppressed, or privileged/disadvantaged. Worrying about things like danger discourse, microaggressions, and implicit bias come from the head and not the heart, and during the first weeks of class, this could make the new teacher's behavior seem contrived and inauthentic, which the kids will notice and respond to immediately.

The best way to bond with new students is to be genuine, honest, and loose, and to have patience and a good sense of humor—all of which are universal behaviors and aren't subject to the rigidity of mechanical intellectual processing. Doing these things will allow the new teacher to forget their nerves and put their attention on helping the kids in their class, not on whether or not they should say or think a certain thing for fear of violating an ideology.

Still, there will be some students that the new teacher will not reach, and these students may act out; in certain cases, there could be some anxiety-provoking negative behavior. And pretending that this challenging and in certain cases violent behavior is simply a myth, or a distortion of reality perpetuated by a white racial frame, will not give the student-teacher the skills and understanding necessary to be an effective educator. Future teachers need to know that violence in urban schools may be a real challenge they face, and that many urban children are caught in the cycle of poverty, which does disproportionately affect students of color.

Future educators must know that *poverty is not a culture*, however, and that assuming this *is* a cause for concern. As educator and writer Zaretta Hammond states in her successful education text, *Culturally Responsive Teaching & the Brain*, coping skills are often mistaken for norms and beliefs. Hammond writes:

> What appears to be "culture"—norms, beliefs, and behaviors that are transmitted from one generation to another—are more accurately coping and survival mechanisms that help marginalized communities navigate what Alexander in *The New Jim Crow* calls racial and economic caste systems. The experiences of African Americans and Latinos living in poverty is no different than the experience of those living though the Great Depression or major military conflicts. The only difference is those experiences were temporary, so the coping mechanisms did not become codified.[11]

Hammond acknowledges that negative behaviors by students of color in urban schools are real, but that they are not normalized and are separate from culture. "Often these behaviors are an outgrowth of post-traumatic stress disorder (PTSD)," Hammond writes, offering research from Stanford's Early Life Stress Research Program that showed "as many as one-third of children living in our country's urban neighborhoods have PTSD—nearly twice the rate reported for troops returning from war zones in Iraq."[12]

Which is why these behaviors must be acknowledged and unpacked, not ignored or blamed on racist distortions in an attempt to forward identity politics.

THE COURAGE OF TRANSPARENCY

Violence in urban schools is not a mythological outgrowth of danger discourse, or the result of distorted thinking by racist whites. Education advocates and school reformers understand this, as do journalists working to uncover and document the challenges that exist in America's biggest districts. In April 2012, the *Philadelphia Inquirer* won a Pulitzer Prize in the category of Public Service for its series on school violence in Philadelphia public schools titled "Assault on Learning."

Specifically, the *Inquirer* won "for its exploration of pervasive violence in the city's schools, using powerful print narratives and videos to illuminate crimes committed by children against children and to stir reforms to improve safety for teachers and students."[13] Put another way, journalists John Sullivan, Kristin Graham, Sue Snyder, and Dylan Purcell of the *Inquirer* won because they worked to put the disinfectant of sunlight on the crime and violence in Philadelphia schools that not only made students and teachers unsafe, but also ruined the educations of countless children, especially those of color; the student population of the School District of Philadelphia is over 70 percent black and Latino.

The first article in the *Inquirer*'s "Assault on Learning" series, headlined "Climate of Violence Stifles City Schools," gave an overview of the depth and breadth of their investigation:

> The Inquirer spent a year looking into violence in Philadelphia public schools, interviewing hundreds of teachers, parents, students, and education experts about the district's problems. It also commissioned an extensive, independently administered survey by Temple University that sampled the opinions of more than 750 teachers and aides—6 percent of the 13,000 the district employs. . . .
>
> The Inquirer also obtained thousands of internal School District police reports of violent incidents dating back to 2007. They show that during the last four years serious crimes occurred dozens of times a day, in every corner of the city, at every level of school. Case histories of assaults that landed in Common Pleas Court were reviewed . . . and a database was created with information provided by the School District and analyzed, detailing more than 30,000 serious incidents—from assaults to robberies to rapes—reported in the district during the last five years.[14]

Tragically, many of the victims of this violence were students of color. Like Teshada Herring of Audenried High School, who was attacked on January 22, 2010, by a gang of fellow students while she was in the middle of class taking an algebra test. According to the *Inquirer*:

> Suddenly, a band of more than a dozen girls and boys—captured on video roaming the halls and looking into classrooms—barged through the door. The group converged on Teshada and began to beat her. In less than a minute, they vanished. "It was like a tornado," her teacher would later say. "They went one way, then they went the other way. In Philadelphia, schools are no sanctuary. The Jan. 22, 2010, assault on Teshada, which left her bleeding and dazed, was the 2,095th violent incident the School District recorded in the 2009-10 year.[15]

Only minutes after the assault on Teshada, a security camera revealed a second assault happening in the school. A dozen students surrounded a tenth-grade girl and began punching and kicking her, even though she lay helpless on the floor. The girl suffered a serious eye injury, and one of the students charged in the attack broke her finger in the fight. School security guards were barely able to react quick enough to break up the incident, as some of them were still already dealing with the assault on Teshada.

The violence that day didn't end there. Tragically, later that night, a South Philadelphia High athlete named Tyree Parks was shot to death while walking home from an Audenried youth basketball game. At the crime scene, police found Tyree had been carrying a .32-caliber semiautomatic handgun.[16]

Audenried wasn't the only school in a predominantly black neighborhood that had serious safety issues documented by the *Inquirer*. In the weeks following the assault on Teshada Herring, a gang fight at Simon Gratz High in North Philadelphia put a student in the hospital with a broken eye socket. At Heston Elementary in West Philadelphia, a sixth grader was arrested for bringing a gun to class. And at Bregy Elementary in South Philadelphia, a fifth grader sexually assaulted a female classmate by grabbing her by the head and grinding on her.[17]

One of the most troubling parts of the *Inquirer* investigation was that it uncovered children—ages five to ten—assaulting staff and classmates. In October 2010 at Dobson Elementary in Manayunk, a classroom assistant was "spat on, punched and kicked—all by a kindergartner. The aide suffered torn ligaments and tendons in a hand." During that same month at Southwark Elementary in South Philadelphia, a ten-year-old boy "body slammed into his teacher with such force that she suffered a concussion as she fell to the ground."

In April 2008 at Taylor Elementary in Hunting Park, a third grade child "held a knife against a classmate's throat and threatened to cut off his head if he snitched." And in February of 2008 at Morris Elementary in North Philadelphia, "an angry 9-year-old punched his pregnant teacher in the stomach."[18]

From 2005–2006 to 2009–2010, more than 4,000 teacher assaults were reported. As detailed in the *Inquirer* story headlined "Violence targets teachers, staff,":

> Veteran Philadelphia school teacher Lou Austin endured 40 minutes of terror as the 15-year-old ninth grader jabbed his index finger into Austin's temple and threatened to kill him while swinging a pair of scissors menacingly. Austin didn't even know the youth, who ransacked his classroom—flipping desks and attempting to set fire to books—at Lincoln High School in Mayfair on Valentine's Day. He'd merely asked him to step away from his classroom door and go to his own class when the youth exploded. Austin's experience illustrates

the dangers and frustration that teachers in Philadelphia public schools face daily.[19]

Many teachers ended up quitting, which left some of the city's most vulnerable students without a stable learning environment. Sean Fennessy, a former teacher at Olney High School East, witnessed a brutal attack on a student in his classroom in March 2010. A male student rushed into his room and beat up another boy. According to the *Inquirer*, "the victim fell to the floor between two desks. His attacker had time to throw 20 to 30 punches before fleeing." Fennessy quit in June, three months later.[20]

By June 2010, the total number of violent incidents during the 2009–2010 school year had grown to 4,541, which meant an average of 25 a day. Such violence traumatized students and teachers alike, and took a serious toll on learning. Arlene C. Ackerman, the superintendent at the time, said school violence was a national public health problem, stating, "We're going to have to fix it as a collective effort and not expect the school to take on the responsibility for trying to do everything."[21]

Such efforts are still needed today. In November 2019, NBC10 Philadelphia published a survey it gave to 3,000 Philadelphia public school teachers which consisted of 18 questions related to workplace safety, among other issues. Of the 511 teachers who responded, 61 percent said that they did not believe that their school was "well protected against potential violence whether it be internal or external," and nearly 50 percent said that they "witness students physically assaulting one another" either daily or weekly. When asked "have you ever been physically assaulted by a student?", 150 teachers said yes, which was almost 30 percent of the respondents.[22]

Teaching in urban school districts can be challenging, and the anxiety new teachers face is very real. The unease felt by student-teachers from "sheltered" suburban neighborhoods, who do not have the experience dealing with diverse students in big cities, should be acknowledged and validated, not deemed a "distortion" coming from a white racial frame. Only by taking an honest look at the issues plaguing urban schools will real change take place.

DEDICATED TO POSITIVE CHANGE

Despite all the challenges facing urban schools, many teachers have stayed the course and dedicated their careers to making a positive difference in their students' lives. Scores of hard-working educators from nearly every part of the city—from Somerton in the far northeast to Eastwick in southwest—have stayed put in their classrooms day after day, year after year, molding the minds of young people and setting a positive example, teaching with passion and enthusiasm, going beyond the call of duty and spending thousands of their own dollars on school supplies and equipment to make their lessons the best they can be.

Culinary arts teachers have helped their students win $50,000 scholarships to the nations' top culinary schools, and construction technology instructors have gotten their kids into trade unions before graduating high school; drama teachers have built entire stages and sets from scratch, and put on a school play for a crowd of 500; and journalism teachers have helped students produce school newspapers entirely from their own laptops.

Algebra teachers, in an effort to help kids pass the Pennsylvania Keystone Exam, have personally delivered homework to the houses of students who were absent from school; track and field coaches have turned school hallways into long jump runways, and parking lots into multi-lane tracks; and counselors have guided students through the stages of grief after losing a parent to suicide or a drug overdose.

The thing that all these dedicated men and women have in common is that they are *there for their students*, through the ups and downs, highs and lows, good times and bad. It sounds cliché, but the sad fact is that for many of these children, the teacher or coach is the only constant in their lives, as things like domestic violence, substance abuse, and economic factors prevent any long-term stability from their family, and they bounce from mother, to father, to grandparent, and back again.

Tragically, some Philadelphia students don't even have a family at all. Like Santo McCloskey, who in May 2016, was a five-year-old little boy without a home. This forced teachers from Willard Elementary School in the Kensington section of the city to become his surrogate family. Apparently, the boy was getting himself to school, but then waiting around at the end of the day, not knowing who was going to pick him up.

"I would clean him up every day in the morning," said Penny Hlat, Santo's kindergarten teacher at the time. "He was just a child, you could tell he needed a lot more love and support than he was getting." Then the Department of Human Services arrived one afternoon, asking someone to take him in. Schoolteacher Kelly McCloskey did just that, and by 7:00 that night, he had a new home. In December 2019, Santo was officially adopted by McCloskey and her husband.[23]

Educators in Philadelphia are indeed making a difference. Like Debontina Adamson-White, a sixth grade teacher at Harding Middle School, who was the School District of Philadelphia's Teacher of the Month for November 2019. "She is an advocate for her students and focuses on individualized instruction to highlight the potential of each student she teaches," said nominator and colleague Blair Downie. "She is able to teach her students how to succeed and make a positive impact in their communities. Debontina has an infections character that has had a positive impact on the climate and culture of our building!"[24]

And with the help of dedicated teachers, the violence and bad behavior in schools is improving. Like at Hartranft Elementary in North Philadelphia, whose use of Positive Behavior Interventions and Supports (PBIS) is changing the culture of the building for the better. As reported by the *Inquirer*:

> At Hartranft, a 500-student school at Seventh and Cumberland Streets, discipline used to work the way it worked in schools for years: Kids were expected to behave, and if they didn't, they were punished. Positive behavior supports is a proactive strategy: It's about teaching students very specifically what good behavior looks like in the hallway, in the cafeteria, in the schoolyard, and then reinforcing it with rewards. (At Hartranft, kids earn Panther Paws, which they can redeem for trinkets or buy experiences like pizza parties or field trips.) . . .
>
> PBIS came to Hartranft in 2012. The shift was slow, but it gained steam when [principal] Lytle came to the school four years ago. The school's credo—Be safe! Be respectful! Be responsible!—is everywhere, and even the youngest student can tell you exactly what that means.[25]

As a result of PBIS, Hartranft's suspensions and discipline referrals went down. Attendance and academics improved, too. According to Philadelphia's School Performance Report (SPR), which takes into account academics, climate, and college and career readiness, the school went from 7 out of 100 in 2014–2015, to a 42 in 2016–2017. Average SPR scores have gone up across the city as well. As a whole, school district and charter schools in 2018–2019 scored an average of 44 out of 100 possible points. The prior year, the average was 42; the average score was only 33 in 2014–2015.[26]

Interestingly, alongside its many challenges, the School District of Philadelphia has a proud history of both academic and athletic achievement. Julia R. Masterman Laboratory and Demonstration School, located only six blocks from the Philadelphia Museum of Art, is perhaps the city's best kept secret. In 2019, *U.S. News & World Report* ranked Masterman's secondary program the #1 high school in Pennsylvania, and with a 100 percent graduation rate and 87 college readiness score, was listed #22 in the nation.[27]

Although Masterman's success is known to Philadelphians—especially to ambitious parents looking to get the best education for their children—not many people outside the city know that Masterman regularly has the highest SAT scores in the state, or that their middle school program won back-to-back National Junior High chess championships in 2013 and 2014.[28]

Masterman isn't the only academic gem in Philadelphia. Central High School, whose notable alumni include Noam Chomsky, Bill Cosby, and Philadelphia's first black mayor, Wilson Goode Jr., was ranked #4 in the state in 2019. Other successful schools in Philadelphia include Academy at Palumbo (#43), Carver High School (#61), Girard Academic Music Program (#67), William W. Bodine High School (#69), and Girls High School (#97). Although the Philadelphia School for Creative and Performing Arts isn't in the top 100 in Pennsylvania (it's #117 out of 673), they can boast of being the home school of Boyz II Men, the widely popular and award-winning R&B group who played the Super Bowl in 1998.

Other famous graduates of Philadelphia public schools include actors Kevin Bacon (Masterman '76) and Will Smith (Overbrook '86); singer Patti Labelle (Bartram '61); three-time Olympic gold medalist and American Hall of Fame Basketball player Dawn Staley (Dobbins '88); actor and comedian Kevin Hart (George Washington '97); and NBA legend Wilt Chamberlain (Overbrook '55), among many others.

It's not just famous alumni that make Philadelphia proud, but also the everyday unsung men and women who've attended Philly's public schools, like accountant Melvin Pitts, who graduated Benjamin Franklin High School in 1996; schoolteacher Terrance Williams, who graduated Overbrook in 2001; nurse Priscilla Núñez, who graduated Edison High School in 2003; and investment accountant John Hardin-Bey, who graduated Abraham Lincoln High School in 2005.[29]

Educators who spend their careers in Philadelphia will end up meeting thousands of amazing young men and women who have worked hard and made their teachers and families proud. They will see that kids from all races and backgrounds have been able to achieve success—some going on to college, the military, or straight into the trade unions—and many will come back years later to thank them and share their stories.

And these are human stories that all people can relate to—free from the dualism of identity politics—stories rooted in pride, determination, and love.

RECOMMENDATIONS

1. The concept of "colorblindness" should be consistent across all cultures and ethnicities. If antiracists preach that acknowledging the importance of race is needed to bring about positive change, then race should be acknowledged in all areas of society, including statistics on neighborhood crime and school violence, as sunlight is the best disinfectant.

2. Violence in urban schools is not a mythological outgrowth of danger discourse, or the result of distorted thinking by racist whites. The idea that danger discourse "distorts reality, trivializes the true direction of violence and positions whites as innocent" is also questionable, because it suggests that the discourse is false or exaggerated, when in fact it may not be. Further, suggesting that such realities are not the "true" direction of violence is a cause for concern, being that violence—no matter what the cause—is not acceptable, even if such violence stems in part from institutional racism.

3. Future teachers need to know that violence in urban schools may be a real challenge they face, and that many urban children are caught in the cycle

of poverty, which does disproportionately affect students of color. Future educators must know that *poverty is not a culture*, however, and that assuming this *is* a cause for concern.

4. The best way for teachers to bond with new students is to be genuine, honest, and loose, and to have patience and a good sense of humor—all of which are universal behaviors and aren't subject to the rigid and mechanical intellectual processing of antiracism. Doing these things will allow the new teacher to forget their nerves and put their attention on helping the kids in their class, not on whether or not they should say or think a certain thing for fear of violating a political ideology.

NOTES

1. Robin DiAngelo, *What Does It Mean to Be White?: Developing White Cultural Literacy Revised* (New York: Peter Lang, 2016), 277–282.
2. Ibid., 278.
3. Ibid., 183.
4. Ibid., 279.
5. Ibid., 278.
6. Ibid., 129–130.
7. Heather Mac Donald, "Police Shootings and Race," *Washington Post*, July 18, 2016, https://www.washingtonpost.com (accessed January 22, 2020).
8. Robin DiAngelo, *What Does It Mean to Be White?*, 278.
9. Ibid.
10. Heather Mac Donald, "Police Shootings and Race."
11. Zaretta Hammond, *Culturally Responsive Teaching & the Brain: Promoting Authentic Engagement and Rigor among Culturally and Linguistically Diverse Students* (Thousand Oaks, CA: Corwin, 2015), 32–33.
12. Ibid.
13. The Pulitzer Prizes, The 2012 Pulitzer Prize Winner in Public Service, https://www.pulitzer.org (accessed February 4, 2020).
14. John Sullivan, Susan Snyder, Kristen A. Graham, and Dylan Purcell, "Climate of Violence Stifles City Schools," *Philadelphia Inquirer*, March 27, 2011.
15. Ibid.
16. Ibid.
17. Ibid.
18. Susan Snyder, John Sullivan, Kristen A. Graham, and Dylan Purcell, "Children Ages 5 to 10 Assault Staff and Classmates. Some Commit Sex Offenses," *Philadelphia Inquirer*, March 29, 2011.
19. Susan Snyder, Kristen A. Graham, John Sullivan, and Dylan Purcell, "Violence Targets Teachers, Staff," *Philadelphia Inquirer*, March 30, 2011.
20. Ibid.
21. Ibid.
22. "'There Will Be No Teachers Left': Educators in Philadelphia Talk about Quitting, School Violence and Paying for Classroom Supplies," NBC10 Philadelphia, February 4, 2020, https://www.nbcphiladelphia.com (accessed February 11, 2020).
23. Beccah Hendrickson, "Heartwarming: Teacher Adopts Student from Philadelphia School," 6ABC Action News, December 19, 2019, https://www.6abc.com (accessed February 12, 2020).
24. Teachers of the Month for October and November, The School District of Philadelphia, November 26, 2019, https://www.philasd.org/ (accessed February 12, 2020).

25. Kristen A. Graham, "How Philly Schools Are Cutting Out Bad Behavior and Improving Academics," *Philadelphia Inquirer*, February 16, 2018, https://www.inquirer.com (accessed February 12, 2020).

26. Maddie Hanna and Kristen A. Graham, "Which Are the Best, Most Improved Philly Schools? District Reveals Them," *Philadelphia Inquirer*, February 10, 2020 https://www.inquirer.com, (accessed February 12, 2020).

27. "Best Pennsylvania High Schools," *U.S. News & World Report*, 2019, https://www.usnews.com (accessed February 2, 2020).

28. David Chang, "Philly Chess Team Wins Back-to-Back National Titles," NBC 10 Philadelphia, April 30, 2014, https://www.nbcphiladelphia.com (accessed February 2, 2020).

29. "Success Stories," Philadelphia Futures, https://philadelphiafutures.org (accessed February 2, 2020).

Chapter Seven

Racial Disparities and School Discipline

Following the lead of the Obama administration's 2014 "Dear Colleague" letter—which issued guidance to public schools aimed at eliminating so-called discriminatory student discipline practices—whiteness scholars have used disparate-impact theory to interpret racial disparities in school discipline as evidence of racial discrimination.[1] Simply stated, whiteness scholars preach that if the rates of things like school suspensions and expulsions are not proportionate among the races, it can only mean one thing: racism.

In July 2019, the United States Commission on Civil Rights released a briefing report titled, "Beyond Suspensions: Examining School Discipline Policies and Connections to the School-to-Prison Pipeline for Students of Color with Disabilities," which argued that black students are disciplined more than whites because of disparities in treatment, not because of disparities in behavior. Peter Kirsanow (who is African American) and Gail Heriot, two members of the U.S. Commission on Civil Rights, disagreed with the report and issued written dissents. Kirsanow stated:

> One of the defects in this report is that it starts from the assumption that disparate outcomes between groups of students are the consequence of discriminatory behavior on the part of teachers and school administrators. To put it another way, the report assumes that all children enter school on a trajectory of academic success and good behavior, but this trajectory is interrupted by teachers and administrators who discriminate against students on the basis of race, disability, and so on. The discriminatory behavior redirects a student's natural trajectory toward academic failure and eventual imprisonment. The assumption is unsupported by the evidence.[2]

Kirsanow went on to explain that "children do not enter school as blank slates," and that the stability of home life—where kids learn academic and social skills that impact study habits and behavior regulation—vary greatly among children.

He also referenced data based on the Early Childhood Longitudinal Study, Kindergarten Class (ECLS-K) of 1998–1999 which showed that "odds differentials in suspensions are likely produced by pre-existing behavioral problems of youth that are imported into the classroom, that cause classroom disruptions, and that trigger disciplinary measures by teachers and school officials," and that differences in rates of suspension between racial groups "appear to be a function of differences in problem behaviors that emerge early in life, that remain relatively stable over time, and that materialize in the classroom."[3]

Commissioner Gail Heriot also dissented from the report, stating "never before has the Commission so seriously misunderstood the empirical research that purportedly forms the basis for its conclusions." One conclusion drawn from the report was as follows: *Students of color as a whole, as well as by individual racial group, do not commit more disciplinable offenses than their white peers.* Heriot called this "the most insupportable Finding in the report," writing:

> The report provides no evidence to support this sweeping assertion and there is abundant evidence to the contrary. Not the least of that evidence comes from teachers. When one looks at aggregate statistics concerning which students are sent to the principal's office by their teachers, there are strong differences. Denying those differences amounts to an accusation that teachers are getting it not just wrong, but very wrong. It is a slap in the face to teachers. I wish racial disparities of this kind did not exist. And there is very little I wouldn't give to make them disappear. But the evidence shows they do exist, and pretending otherwise doesn't benefit anyone (with the possible exception of identity politics activists). It certainly does not benefit minority children. To the contrary, they are its greatest victims.[4]

As Commissioner Heriot notes in her dissent, the report marginalizes data from teachers—the men and women who are at the center of school discipline issues in their own classrooms and schools. Acknowledging such data would clearly reveal that all student behavior isn't the same. Still, even self-reported data shows racial differences in student conduct. Since 1993, the National Center for Education Statistics has asked students in grades nine through twelve every other year whether they have been in a physical fight on school property over the past twelve months. Consistently, more black students have reported participating in fights than white students.[5]

According to Commissioner Heriot:

In 2015, 12.6% of African American students reported being in a fight on school property, as contrasted with 5.6% of white students. Put differently, the African American rate was 125% higher than the white rate. Similarly, in 2013, 12.8% of African American students reported being in a fight on school property and 6.4% of white students did. Back in the 1990s, the number of students reported participating in a fight on school property was generally higher. But the racial gaps were just as real. In 1993, 22% of African American students and 15% of white students admitted to participating in such a fight.[6]

Asian American students, on the other hand, had lower rates of participation in fights on school property than whites did. In 2005, the rate was 5.9 percent for Asians, and 11.6 percent for whites.[7]

So why do racial disparities exist in school discipline? It's a complex issue to say the least. Differences in things like poverty, parental education, books in the home, television watching, nutrition, father absenteeism, and the injustices of systemic racism and policy failures all play a part. But as Commissioner Heriot writes, "Whatever the genesis of these disparities, they need to be dealt with realistically. We don't live in a make believe world."[8]

THE SCHOOL-TO-PRISON PIPELINE

Whiteness scholar Robin DiAngelo speaks of racial arrogance in much of her writing, insisting that because white people are not educated about racism in schools and society, they are racially illiterate.[9] She's also fond of referring to something known as the School-to-Prison Pipeline (STPP), which is the notion that it's white teachers and administrators in schools—in combination with a broken criminal justice system and an uncaring network of social services agencies—who are responsible for channeling young people of color into prison, *not* absent fathers or the cycle of poverty, or the numerous other family and societal factors that cause young children to develop violent and inappropriate behaviors as a coping strategy in school.

In particular, she highlights the fact that black students are over three times more likely to be suspended from school than their white counterparts, and repeats the falsehood debunked by U.S. Civil Rights Commissioners Kirsanow and Heriot that black conduct exhibited in schools is no different than white or Asian behavior. She also says that American schools are criminalizing children of color instead of educating them, and that the racial disparity in discipline is a result of "a predominantly white, middle-class, and suburban teaching force that does not understand and often fears people of color and disproportionately sends black and Latino youth to special education and punishes them more harshly than white students for the same offenses."[10]

For schoolteachers who have dedicated their entire lives to teaching Philadelphia youth of all races and ethnic backgrounds, there's nothing more "racially arrogant" than a whiteness scholar—with an all-white background and upbringing and who teaches in an all-white affluent college community—telling them they are creating a "pipeline to prison" for their students. In fact, the whole STPP concept—which once again is heavy on identity politics and light on hard data from inside real urban classrooms and schools—is one of the most arrogant, divisive, and demoralizing perspectives on American education that an urban schoolteacher will ever encounter. As Commissioner Heriot wrote in her dissent, it is "a slap in the face to teachers."

Sadly, as a result of whiteness studies, this is what America's future educators are being taught—that a white teaching force is criminalizing students of color and channeling them to prison. Does some institutional racism still exist in American schools? No question. Is a history of segregation having an impact on teachers, schools, and students of color? Without a doubt.

But such systemic issues are only part of the problem, and they are not insurmountable; blacks have the capability to overcome these obstacles on their own, despite whiteness scholars' patronizing claim that white society must first dismantle the institutions that make it impossible for blacks to succeed. As such, college kids should not be taught in whiteness courses that American institutions work together to create predictable social outcomes such as STPP, and that this systemic social oppression is so powerful, adept and elusive that it can't be isolated to a single person or act, as DiAngelo insists.[11]

The concepts at the heart of STPP are identical to all the others in whiteness studies, in that they are conveniently protected against opposing points of view. Like with the notion of race itself, which exists as a "social construct" when it's needed politically, and disappears into thin air when it's challenged on the basis of culture or genetics. Because the idea of STPP is "systemic" and thus invisible, no one person or act is to blame, which nullifies the idea of personal responsibility, and thus alleviates the need for quantitative, individually documented cases of racism or discrimination, and is why the U.S. Commission on Civil Rights could issue a report contrary to the very real experiences of teachers in American classrooms.

On one hand, whiteness scholars insist racism is real and pervasive, and that justice must be served, yet on the other, the perpetrators of this racism are either ambiguous "systems" which can't be held personally accountable, or are individuals who are acting "unconsciously" via implicit biases and microaggressions, rendering a person's intentions meaningless. In either case, the "racism" is vague and often unseen by the "racist," and many times can only be identified by antiracists and whiteness scholars themselves; the whole concept is dangerously close to what was known as "spectral evidence" in the Salem Witch Trials.

No one can ever get pinned down with any real accountability, because once this happens, racial inequality goes from "systemic" to personal, and then members of so-called oppressed groups would also be responsible for finding solutions, and intentions would once again have meaning. This doesn't serve the function of identity politics. Whiteness scholars need to have the ability to lambast all whites as "racist," and preach that whiteness is oppressive, dominant, and intentionally creating systems of injustice in an effort to hoard social capital, while at the same time, avoid being accused of maligning entire groups of people.

Whiteness scholars can criticize, judge, and call whole groups names associated with hatred and genocide (like "racist" and "white supremacist"), and insist that America's teachers and schools are sending poor black kids to prison (as with "STPP"), yet sit back and smile, insisting it's okay, don't worry, privileged whites who unknowingly perpetuate oppression are still good people, as the "good/bad binary" of racism isn't real.

DiAngelo piggybacks off writer and law professor Michelle Alexander's idea that Jim Crow has not ended, but has simply been redesigned so that it accomplishes the same segregated and racially unjust outcomes.[12] The notion that there exists a system independent of individual intentions and personal responsibility—a system *intentionally* designed to oppress people of color—is debatable.

Still, teaching America's future educators to see the world via this lens can be counterproductive, and is doing little to directly help those in need. As for preaching that America's hard working teachers are creating a pipeline to prison for their students, there's no better way to suck the life out of public schools, and to further tarnish a profession that's already struggling to meet the educational challenges of the twenty-first century.

RACE-BASED DISCIPLINE

The 2014 "Dear Colleague" letter jointly issued by the U.S. Department of Education and the U.S. Department of Justice had a significant impact on school discipline in American public schools, forcing districts to change their discipline policies in an effort to comply with the new federal guidelines to avoid being investigated or prosecuted for civil rights violations. The purpose of the letter was to "assist public elementary and secondary schools in meeting their obligations under Federal law to administer student discipline without discriminating on the basis of race, color, or national origin," being that "students of certain racial or ethnic groups tend to be disciplined more than their peers."[13]

The letter argued that the disparities in discipline were not the result of differences in behavior, but of racial discrimination, stating "research suggests that the substantial racial disparities of the kind reflected in the CRDC data are not explained by more frequent or more serious misbehavior by students of color." Again, this conclusion is debatable, as Peter Kirsanow and Gail Heriot, two members of the U.S. Commission on Civil Rights, have recently documented in their written dissents of the 2019 STPP briefing. Still, the "Dear Colleague" letter took an antiracist approach in that it ultimately viewed any racial disparity in school discipline as evidence of racism, even if policies were fair and applied evenly across all races.

This is where the concept of disparate-impact comes into play. According to the letter, "Schools also violate Federal law when they evenhandedly implement facially neutral policies and practices that, although not adopted with the intent to discriminate, nonetheless have an unjustified effect of discriminating against students on the basis of race."[14]

Which simply means that if school discipline data isn't proportionate among the races, discrimination has taken place. In other words, the letter falls victim to the fallacy that *correlation implies causation*, which finds a relationship between two variables exists, but erroneously concludes that one variable *causes* the other. Because 85 percent of America's teachers are white, and discipline disparities are adversely affecting students of color, this must mean that racism is taking place—or that the white teachers are *causing* the disparities.

Although this may be true in some instances, the correlation could be attributed to a lurking variable, which is a third factor that may be causing the relationship. A classic example of a lurking variable is the correlation between ice cream sales and drowning: as ice cream sales go up, so do drownings. Does ice cream cause drowning? Of course not. There's a lurking variable—hot weather. Are white teachers causing the disparities in discipline among the races? Although whiteness scholars insist they are, there could be a lurking variable: *student behavior*.

As noted, this is a major point of contention. Do students of different races misbehave at different rates? It's clearly documented that there are major differences among the races in things like family structure and parent participation at school, class size, school safety, hunger and nutrition, frequent school changing, teacher absence and turnover, access to books, television watching, exposure to lead, and summer achievement gain/loss, among other things.[15]

Yet in light of these realities, whiteness scholars and other social justice advocates still insist that kids of all races exhibit nearly identical conduct in school, that somehow children who are exposed to domestic violence and substance abuse in the home—and who attend schools with safety issues and regularly sit in classes with substitute teachers—*have no significant difference in behavior*.

The insistence on such things is more about identity politics and political correctness than rational inquiry. The research that suggests there is no difference in student behavior has been debunked by the anecdotal observations of teachers themselves, and by civil rights Commissioners like Kirsanow and Heriot. Yet the movement to pretend that all students, regardless of home environment and the quality of schools, behave the same is a growing one, because suggesting otherwise is considered too dangerous for society to handle, as such information could be used to further oppress people of color.

This leads to the concept of "disparate-impact" in the 2014 "Dear Colleague" letter, and the notion that racism will only cease to exist when the data shows that students of all races are disciplined proportionately. Interestingly, the actual behavior of the students isn't the primary concern of school districts. Rather, it is the way in which this data are reported to the federal government.

As Peter Kirsanow writes in his *National Review* article titled, "Racial Disparities and School Discipline," which details his argument against the findings of the 2019 STPP briefing report:

> The trouble with the Commission's approach is that when you decree, in the face of all evidence to the contrary (including the testimony of their own parents), that children of all racial groups misbehave at exactly the same rates, the only way to get discipline rates to be the same is to artificially depress them. Accordingly, misbehaving students aren't suspended or expelled, they're invited to take part in "restorative practices" and "positive behavioral interventions and supports."[16]

So in essence, that's what the 2014 "Dear Colleague" letter accomplished: it artificially depressed discipline rates by limiting the suspensions and expulsions of students of color. Specifically, African American and Latino males, who were three times as likely to be removed from classrooms as their white counterparts. Granted, there were some very real advantages to keeping these children in classrooms with their peers, and the alternative discipline approaches used instead of suspensions—such as restorative justice and positive behavior interventions and supports—did have some genuine value, and indeed made a positive change in certain cases.

However, as noted by Kirsanow, behavior reform was secondary to data manipulation, as America's public schools first and foremost wanted to comply with the new federal guidelines to avoid the wrath of the DOJ. In some schools in the Philadelphia School District, the pressure from central office administrators to keep school disciplinarians from formally suspending male students of color was quite real, and in certain instances, the learning environment was compromised as a result.

But Philadelphia was hardly alone in this situation, as public schools across America were experiencing some very challenging effects from what some have called a disastrous discipline policy that robbed numerous children—many of whom were students of color—of their right to an education.

DISCIPLINE THROUGH THE EYES OF TEACHERS

In July 2019, right around the time the U.S. Commission on Civil Rights released their STPP briefing, the Fordham Institute published their own analysis of public school discipline policies called "Discipline Reform through the Eyes of Teachers," which documented the actual classroom experiences and anecdotal observations of America's educators concerning the effects of the "Dear Colleague" letter, instead of discrediting and discounting such information.[17]

Although the report didn't directly address whether or not disparities in discipline were the result of disparities in behavior, it did conclude that the rescinding of the "Dear Colleague" letter guidelines in December 2018 by U.S. Education Secretary Betsy DeVos was a right move. In their foreword, the Fordham Institute report stated:

> Federal policymakers issue a new mandate with the goal of improving schools, especially for poor kids and students of color, but by the time it migrates from the capital to the statehouse and from there to local school boards, to central offices, to principals, to other administrators, and (finally) to teachers in an elaborate game of telephone, much has changed—and almost never for the better. It's the challenge of implementation in a huge, loosely coupled, and mostly fragmented "system" like America's K–12 education.
>
> We worried that something like this was happening with school discipline. Reformers' goal was to prod schools toward alternatives to suspensions and expulsions by improving school climate, fostering more engaging teaching, adopting restorative practices, and the like. But we surmised that on the ground (in real schools) teachers would simply be told that students couldn't be disciplined like they used to be—and that they'd be on their own when it came to dealing with the consequences. Contrary to the assumptions of many reformers, that might be bad for the disruptive students themselves, and it would almost certainly be bad for their well-behaved peers, their teachers, and the larger goal of helping students learn.[18]

The report set out to see if these concerns were valid. In particular, it sought the input from teachers who were forced to deal with the consequences of the "Dear Colleague" discipline guidelines in their own classrooms and schools. It surveyed a nationally representative sample of 1,200 African American and white teachers in elementary and high school classrooms about school discipline, a study which the Fordham Institute billed as the "first scientifically rigorous and nationally representative survey on school discipline to be published in at least a decade and a half." Fordham also noted that it was also the first time a discipline survey had included a specific focus on the views of African American teachers and teachers in high-poverty schools.[19]

The results were eye-opening. One major finding was that teachers in high-poverty schools (where at least 75 percent of students were eligible for federally subsidized lunches) reported more verbal disrespect, physical fighting, and assault—and most said that a disorderly or unsafe environment made learning difficult.[20]

Specifically, teachers in high-poverty schools were twice as likely to say that verbal disrespect was a daily occurrence in their classrooms, six times as likely to say that physical fighting was a daily or weekly occurrence, and three times as likely to report being personally assaulted by a student, as compared to teachers in low-poverty schools (where fewer than 25 percent of students were eligible for federally subsidized lunches).[21]

Interestingly, 60 percent of African American teachers and 57 percent of white teachers in high-poverty schools said that issues with student behavior made learning difficult, suggesting that perceptions of school climate were not racially biased.

The fact that teachers in high-poverty schools reported more problems with behavior is telling, because it reveals that student behavior is indeed influenced by things like poverty, school safety, teacher stability, and so on. And because African Americans on a whole are three times as poor as whites—and have less access to quality schools with experienced teachers, safe environments, and low class sizes—it's not surprising that they would exhibit more challenging behaviors than their white counterparts.

This is not to say that such behavior is cultural or race-related, but that African Americans have historically faced (and still face) more challenges than whites, and these challenges sometimes have adverse effects in classrooms. Racial bias from white teachers does play a part in the disparity in discipline between white and black students, but such bias is not *the only reason for the disparity*, as is suggested by antiracists in the field of whiteness studies.

Another finding of the Fordham study was that most teachers said discipline was inconsistent or inadequate, and that underreporting of serious incidents was "rampant," and that the higher tolerance for misbehavior was in part responsible for the recent decline in student suspensions.[22]

In particular, New York City teachers—who were not permitted to suspend students without permission from the central office—were more apt to say that underreporting was responsible for the decline in suspensions. "Students quickly realize there are no consequences for negative behavior," one New York City teacher was quoted in the survey as saying. "As a result, teachers end up dealing with lots of behaviors that would never be acceptable in any other social situation."[23]

Another teacher, not from New York, had this to say:

> During the 2017–18 school year . . . I saw a complete disregard for the safety of both students and teachers in favor of underreporting significant disciplinary actions. This was done to prevent the reports within the system, which can reflect negatively on a school's rating and grade. It led to an increase in behavioral issues because the students understood that there would be no consequences for their actions. The classrooms were often disrupted by this behavior, and many students would communicate their safety concerns, but to no avail.

Another key finding in the Fordham survey was that teachers strongly believed that the majority of their students suffered at the hands of a few chronically disruptive peers. The idea that one bad apple can ruin the bunch is not politically correct in the twenty-first century—as *all* children have the right to a quality education and proper accommodations from the state—but this still doesn't solve the problem of limited time and resources. In other words, when do the educations of the cooperative 90 percent of students come into play, many of whom are children of color? How long should *their* schooling suffer as a result of problem peers who are kept in classrooms because the federal government says it's racist to remove them?

The most interesting finding in the Fordham report was that many African American teachers said suspensions and other forms of exclusionary discipline should be used *more* often, despite the fact that black teachers were slightly more likely to believe that school discipline was racially biased. The Fordham report noted, curiously, that although implicit bias and a perceived lack of cultural competence are at the heart of discussions of racial disproportionality, other factors may be as or more important—such as teacher turnover and experience.

White teachers don't last as long in high-poverty schools as African American teachers do, and newer, less experienced white teachers are common in poor schools with high populations of students of color. Thus, it could be weaker classroom management skills, coupled with poor instruction, that makes misbehavior more likely in white teachers' classrooms—not simply the existence of unconscious racial biases.[24]

RECOMMENDATIONS

1. Whiteness scholars should not be teaching future educators that America's public schools are criminalizing students of color and intentionally channeling them to prison through a reinvented Jim Crow system. This is demoraliz-

ing to educators of all races, and sucks the life out of public schools, further tarnishing a profession that's already struggling to meet the educational challenges of the twenty-first century.

2. Research shows there are major differences among the races when it comes to home environment and access to quality schools. Things like parent participation in education, class size, school safety, teacher absence and turnover, access to books, television watching, exposure to lead, and summer achievement gain/loss, have an effect on student achievement and behavior. As such, whiteness scholars should refrain from insisting students of all races misbehave at exactly the same rates, and instead of blaming racial disparities in school discipline solely on racism, should broaden their focus to include suggested remedies from classroom teachers, whose anecdotal observations provide a badly needed perspective into the everyday reality of American public schools.

3. Student behavior, not race, should be the primary factor in school discipline. Therefore, whiteness scholars should reevaluate their support for the guidelines set forth in the 2014 "Dear Colleague" letter, which encourage limiting suspensions based on skin color. Such policies can lead to the artificial deflation and underreporting of serious behavior infractions, and can compromise the safety and education of all children of all races.

NOTES

1. "Joint 'Dear Colleague' Letter," U.S. Department of Education, Office for Civil Rights, January 8, 2014, https://www2ed.gov (accessed February 14, 2020).
2. "Beyond Suspensions: Examining School Discipline Policies and Connections to the School-to-Prison Pipeline for Students of Color with Disabilities," United States Commission on Civil Rights, July 2019, 192, https://www.usccr.gov (accessed February 15, 2020).
3. Ibid., 194.
4. Ibid., 186.
5. Ibid., 189.
6. Ibid.
7. Ibid.
8. Ibid., 188.
9. Robin DiAngelo, *What Does It Mean to Be White?: Developing White Cultural Literacy Revised* (New York: Peter Lang, 2016), 205.
10. Ibid., 119–120.
11. Ibid., 122.
12. Ibid.
13. "Joint 'Dear Colleague' Letter," https://www2ed.gov (accessed February 14, 2020).
14. Ibid.
15. Paul E. Barton and Richard J. Coley, *Parsing the Achievement Gap II* (Princeton, NJ: Educational Test Service, April, 2009), https://www.ets.org (accessed January 29, 2020).
16. Peter Kirsanow, "Racial Disparities and School Discipline," *National Review*, July 25, 2019, https://www.nationalreview.com (accessed February 18, 2020).
17. David Griffith and Adam Tyner, "Discipline Reform through the Eyes of Teachers," Thomas B. Fordham Institute, July 2019, https://fordhaminstitute.org (accessed November 30, 2019).
18. Ibid., p. 4.

19. Ibid., p. 6.
20. Ibid., p. 9.
21. Ibid.
22. Ibid., p. 26–30.
23. Ibid., 33.
24. Ibid., 48–50.

Chapter Eight

The Power of Expectations

Education in twenty-first-century America can be divided into two fundamental categories: skills-based approaches, and politics-based approaches. For example, if a girl were to take a "math" class in ninth grade, she would most likely learn algebra, and use the order of operations to solve equations—a traditional skills-based approach. On the other hand, if this student were to take a "math studies" class, she might learn how Western European males have used math to oppress women and people of color, and how the term "mathematician" is culturally biased—clearly a politics-based approach.

There are many examples of the latter at the university level, like "gender studies," or "women's studies," or "race studies." Although the word "studies" is used to connote scientific analysis, too often it's little more than smokescreen for political indoctrination. Hence, these courses could easily be called "gender politics," or "women's politics," or "race politics"—courses that are mostly designed to teach students *what* to think, not *how* to think.

So it goes for whiteness studies, which has slowly trickled down into American public education. Not only are core subjects being watered down with social justice curriculum at the K–12 level, but also white preservice teachers are being taught in their college education courses that they must check their privilege and unpack their unconscious racial biases and microaggressions before stepping into a diverse classroom. Megan E. Lynch, an education professor at Penn State University, published an article in the *Journal of Educational Supervision* in 2018, titled, "The Hidden Nature of Whiteness in Education: Creating Active Allies in White Teachers," which exemplifies academia's push to inject identity politics into America's public schools.

According to Lynch, supervisors of preservice teachers should "explicitly name Whiteness and facilitate conversations or open spaces for dialogue on the problematic nature of Whiteness in schooling."[1] Apparently, this will "provide a springboard for supervisors to develop White teachers' capacity to create anti-racist, democratic classrooms," and as a result, there will be "improved learning for all students."[2]

As with white racial identity development (WRID), the ultimate goal is political—to get young preservice teachers to first adopt, and then espouse, the ideology at the heart of antiracism and whiteness studies, which is that colorblindness and individualism are problematic, that whites perpetuate racism by default, and that whiteness left unchecked will result in the continued oppression of people of color.

Interestingly, Lynch's article provides no specific instructional methodology for achieving a "democratic" classroom that will result in "improved learning for all students," and as is so common with whiteness studies and antiracism, her approaches are maddeningly circular and vague: white preservice teachers will ultimately end the oppressive social construct of "whiteness" when they actively choose not to participate in it anymore. This is done by ending their own implicit biases by reflecting on them and actively discussing "whiteness" with their supervisors, which will help preservice teachers understand their own racialized identity and bring about educational equity for the marginalized students in their classrooms.

Specifically, Lynch lists three goals supervisors of preservice teachers should focus on when including "whiteness" in their work: "developing a sociohistorical understanding of race in education; overcoming colorblindness, Whiteness, and the belief in meritocracy; and working within tensions and emotions (as opposed to abandoning or ignoring them)."[3] The first two follow the traditional tenets of whiteness studies, and the third brings in elements of DiAngelo's white fragility—which teaches that when whites are accused of perpetuating racism and oppression, they have the tendency to react emotionally.

Again, outside heavy doses of identity politics, where is the actual instructional methodology preservice teachers can use to build strong lessons and well-managed democratic classrooms that will help all students achieve? In other words, how do they teach actual *math*—not math studies—to a diverse group of students well enough so they can score high on the SATs and master the concepts and skills necessary for them to succeed? The order of operations—multiply, divide, add, subtract—don't depend on the race of the person solving the equation, and don't change according to culture or skin color. What specific instructional strategies do preservice teachers use to teach math to black kids as opposed to white ones?

The answer to such a question is not readily available. It's a slippery slope suggesting teachers use different instructional strategies to teach math to blacks as opposed to whites, which is why such strategies don't exist. If they did, they would undoubtedly be found to be racist and unequal, especially if they didn't produce exactly the same results.

With the exception of the trite and overused strategy of using rap music to teach students of color traditional academic subjects (which is basically a recipe for mush), and of using more group and cooperative instruction for black and Latino kids because they come from "collective" cultures as opposed to "individual" ones, there isn't much an educator can do to differentiate teaching strategies according to race (which again, would be considered racist).

The only thing left for inexperienced preservice teachers to do is incorporate antiracist ideologies into their future lessons, which focus on decentering whiteness, and preach that there is no such thing as universal human values or study skills that can make a child's academic life more manageable; the use of multicultural education, which celebrates diversity and racial unity, is considered too tame by today's whiteness scholars, many of whom prefer the more provocational antiracist approach to ending institutional racism in education.

So whiteness studies advocates, working from an antiracist framework, mostly come from the politics-based camp, as opposed to a skills-based one. As such, they value ideology over methodology, and politics over science. It is a convenient approach to say the least, as it's rooted in eternal finger-pointing and not only offers little in terms of practical methods or strategies for improving instruction and learning, but also manages to evade any real accountability.

After twenty years of increasingly political antiracist education and social justice curriculum, America's schools appear to be getting worse. Again, according to the results of the 2018 Programme for International Student Assessment (PISA) test, which measures what fifteen-year-old students have learned in math, reading, and science, it was revealed that thirty countries outscored U.S. students in math, and that the performance gap between top-performing and lower-performing students was getting bigger, especially in reading.[4]

Even more interesting are the findings of the Educational Testing Service's 2010 policy report *The White-Black Achievement Gap: When Progress Stopped*, which traced America's racial achievement gap from the civil rights era to 2008.[5] The report noted the gap had two periods: one of progress, and one of stagnation. The period of progress ran through the 1970s and 1980s, when the white-black skills gap in reading and math was significantly narrowed. The period of stagnation began in the late 1980s, when the achievement gap leveled off and in some instances, even began to widen.

The stagnation period was perplexing because it affected those born around the late 1960s, a time when equal-rights legislation started putting an end to racial discrimination. Although there are a number of theories as to why the achievement gap stopped closing, the fact that whiteness studies gained prominence in 1987 with the publication of Peggy McIntosh's article, "White Privilege: Unpacking the Invisible Knapsack," is curious, if not coincidental.[6]

Has the birth of whiteness studies—and the constant promotion of so-called white privilege—had an unintended effect on teacher expectations? In 1968, Harvard psychologist Robert Rosenthal and elementary school principal Lenore Jacobson published their groundbreaking book, *Pygmalion in the Classroom: Teacher Expectation and Pupils' Intellectual Development*, which forever changed the way the education community viewed teacher expectations.[7]

Decades of follow-up studies by Rosenthal and other researchers verified and expanded upon the original findings, proving conclusively that teacher expectations—dubbed the "Pygmalion Effect"—have a significant outcome on student achievement. Also known as a "self-fulfilling prophecy," a teacher's perception has a circular flow which helps shape a student's self-concept, which in turn reinforces the way the teacher acts and reacts to the student, which further influences student self-worth.

In other words, if a teacher regards a student as capable, the student will see the teacher as having confidence in them and strive to live up to this perception, which will lead the teacher to believe the student is indeed capable, and will cause the teacher to continue to treat them as such.

Although the goal of antiracist educators is to level the power structure between whites and people of color, the repeated notion that certain racial groups have a higher social status than others may be unintentionally reinforcing such inequality. In her book, *What Does It Mean to Be White?*, DiAngelo preaches that whites are systemically advantaged, while people of color are disadvantaged; that the intellect and character of whites are valued by society and easily celebrated, while the intellect and character of people of color are not valued and easily denigrated; that whites have internalized dominance which lies at the root of their group privilege, and people of color have internalized oppression which lies at the root of their group struggle.

That whites unconsciously believe they are superior, while people of color unconsciously believe they are inferior; that group identity in America is zero-sum, which means whites achieve their privilege and access to resources at the expense of people of color; and that patterns of racism against minoritized groups will continue indefinitely, and are outside the control of any one individual person.[8]

DiAngelo goes as far as to define "white" as the top classification of society's hierarchy, a position which gives whites social and institutional advantages. Likewise, she defines "whiteness" as a term that reinforces white people as inherently superior in society, and grants them material and psychological advantages.[9] Which is why she rails against meritocracy and individualism: because she believes that no matter how hard people of color work, most will not achieve what whites achieve. To believe in individualism and meritocracy would mean accepting the idea that a person is the captain of their own ship, and that what you put in is what you get out.

These concepts are blasphemous to folks like DiAngelo, because they undermine the idea that racism is solely responsible for inequality in America. But a further analysis of the resistance to meritocracy and individualism reveals that those who reject such concepts have already conceded that people of color will not be able to achieve what whites can.

How might novice teachers fresh from college view their students when folks like DiAngelo are repeatedly telling them whites are advantaged, privileged, and internally dominant, and people of color are disadvantaged, minoritized, and internally oppressed? And how are these future educators, especially white teachers who make up over 80 percent of America's teaching force, supposed to react?

In 2018, a group of educational leaders and scholars known as The New Teacher Project (TNTP) published a research report titled "The Opportunity Myth," which also found that teacher expectations have a significant impact on learning and student achievement. TNTP partnered with 5 diverse school districts and observed nearly 1,000 lessons, reviewed 5,000 assignments, analyzed over 20,000 student work samples, and collected nearly 30,000 real-time student surveys.

The report concluded that too many of America's public school students, despite diligently completing their coursework and following the guidance from their teachers, were not graduating at grade-level in many of their subjects, and were woefully unprepared for college and the workforce.[10] In essence, the report stated that the idea that America's students are receiving a quality education that is giving them an opportunity at success is a "myth."

The report identified four keys to a quality education: grade-appropriate assignments; strong instruction; deep student engagement; and high teacher expectations. Although TNTP found that these four things were too often lacking in American classrooms, the offering of grade-appropriate assignments, as well as high teacher expectations, fluctuated by race. In particular, 38 percent of classrooms with mostly students of color never received a single grade-level assignment, as opposed to only 12 percent of classrooms with mostly white students. Similarly, classrooms with mostly white students were 3.6 times more likely to receive grade-appropriate lessons than classrooms with mostly students of color.[11]

The reasons teacher expectations and assignment rigor fluctuated by race are complex, and although TNTP's report did not further analyze these findings, the possibility that whiteness studies is having a negative effect on teacher expectations—that it's perpetuating a cycle it's ironically trying to end—is an idea that must be further explored.

STEREOTYPE THREAT

For years, psychologists believed that people suffering from traumatic events could find relief by revisiting their trauma and openly discussing, writing, and reflecting upon it. Unpacking it, they reasoned, would help people process the baggage in their unconscious, and help them live freer and happier lives. But recently, therapists have found that *not* talking about past trauma can be wise, too. Dr. Carrie Barron, the Director of the Creativity for Resilience Program at Dell Medical School in Austin, Texas, and a member of the faculty of the Columbia College of Physicians and Surgeons, details such an approach in an article for *Psychology Today*.

She explains that some PTSD survivors have reported that re-exposure to trauma through Prolonged Exposure Therapy makes things worse, and instead of gaining control over the event, they deteriorate. Barron writes:

> For some people "going back there," is not useful and can even exacerbate the problem. Steering clear of a treacherous emotional place may be therapeutic. If one survives but still feels damaged, different or deeply changed, maybe the matter was too much or too negative to handle. In some cases, the choice to avoid re-exposure is a healthy instinct. Choosing to focus on the life-affirming action instead of the undermining thought can be a deeply sound decision.[12]

When it comes to antiracist education, the continuous focus on race, institutional oppression, and the problematic dominance of whiteness may become overly negative, and in certain cases, exacerbate the struggles of students of color. As Stanford's Early Life Stress Research Program showed, one in three children living in America's urban neighborhoods have PTSD, which is nearly twice the rate reported for troops returning from Iraq war zones.[13]

And although identity politics are in no way equal to re-exposure therapy in counseling sessions that deal with past incidents of violence, choosing to focus on positive actions instead of zero-sum privilege issues may indeed be a sound decision. In other words, using a more traditional multicultural approach, one that celebrates diverse role models and the unity of the races—instead of harping on the dualism of oppressors/oppressed and privileged/disadvantaged—may produce happier, healthier learners.

The disadvantages of focusing too heavily on race and racism in school are well documented. A condition known as stereotype threat, which DiAngelo has given credence, is an example. Stereotype threat, according to researchers Claude Steele and Joshua Aronson, "refers to being at risk of confirming, as a self-characteristic, a negative stereotype about one's social group."[14] Specifically, research shows that black students perform worse than whites on standardized tests when race is emphasized.

When race is not emphasized, black students perform the same or better than whites. This indicates that academic performance can be harmed by the awareness that one's behavior might be viewed through the lens of race—and the bigger the focus on the identity group, the more vulnerable the students are to stereotype threat.[15]

The existence of stereotype threat is not without controversy. Lee Jussim, a Rutgers University professor and social psychologist, recently challenged the concept, and posted a link on Twitter citing a European Association of Social Psychology study that found "neither an overall effect of stereotype threat on math performance, nor any moderated stereotype effect."[16] This was in response to a Harvard University graduate student who was taken aback that people were actually skeptical about stereotype threat. The student's Twitter handle was Sa-kiera T. J. Hudson, who tweeted:

> People out here thinking stereotype threat don't exist? I believe Evelyn put it best; there are certain phenomena that feel real, and *because* they feel so real they exist in some important sense. Stereotype threat is one of those cases. Wasn't there a replication project?[17]

There have been over 300 experiments on stereotype threat published in peer-reviewed journals with varying results. DiAngelo indeed embraces the concept, associating it with "internalized oppression," which she describes as the process in which people of color are conditioned by society into falsely believing they are inferior to the dominant culture and do not deserve equal access to resources.[18]

Ironically, two of the empirically validated strategies to reduce stereotype threat directly conflict with the tenets of whiteness studies: deemphasizing threatened social identities; and placing an emphasis on individuality. According to an article published in the *Annual Review of Psychology* by Canadian researchers Steven J. Spencer, Christine Logel, and Paul G. Davies, people who are strongly tied to their social identity tend to perform worse on tests:

> Similarly, people tend to be more invested in the evaluative implications of their performance to the extent that the stigmatized identity is central to their self-concept. For example, only women who were highly identified with their gender performed worse than men on a math test that was described as evaluating the abilities of women in general (Schmader 2002). People high in stigma consciousness are also especially vulnerable to underperformance in high-threat conditions because they tend to interpret more events in light of their stigmatized identity (Brown & Pinel 2003).[19]

This is why researchers have suggested moving standard demographic inquiries about ethnicity and gender to the end of a test—because doing so creates identity safety and removes the risk of students being reduced to a negative stereotype targeting a social identity. In other words, remaining colorblind (and gender-blind) before an exam helps women and people of color perform better.[20]

And if doing so before a test helps performance with threatened groups, why not expand this to include all aspects of education, including instruction? Why bring up race or gender at all in a math or science class? Are such skills-based subjects really the place for social justice lessons and identity politicking? Sure, racial and gender stereotypes must be broken down, but at what expense? The SAT scores of women and people of color?

The *Annual Review of Psychology* article also highlighted numerous studies that found that valuing a person's individuality helped reduce stereotype threat. The article stated:

> Self-affirmation has also been shown to effectively reduce the insidious effects of stereotype threat. Participants can be guided to affirm an important value or self-attribute prior to taking a high-threat test. This self-affirmation restores self-integrity (Steele 1988), leading to improved performance (Frantz et al. 2004, Martens et al. 2006, Schimel et al. 2004). To illustrate, Sherman and colleagues (2013) conducted a field experiment in which they had minority students participate in a values affirmation writing exercise during their regular middle-school classes. Those who participated in this self-affirmation exercise earned higher grades than their fellow minority classmates who did not participate.[21]

Although valuing individuality is different from "individualism," the concept is still very similar: it stems from a place of personal empowerment, and operates under the assumption that individuals have enough control over their situation to succeed, despite institutional or group dynamics. In other words, valuing individuality is about content of character, *not* the color of skin or membership in identity groups. And if such a values affirmation writing exercise improved the grades of minority students in middle school, why not expand this to high school and college? Perhaps values *can* transcend race and lead to success, despite what whiteness scholars claim.

Stereotype threat is not settled science, and more research must be done. However, one thing about the concept is clear: harping on the negativities of race and racism doesn't do students of color any good on standardized tests, and tends to hinder their academic performance.

THE AMERICAN DREAM

In the fall of the 2019–2020 school year, as part of a unit on John Steinbeck's *Of Mice and Men*, a Philadelphia English teacher required his tenth grade students to complete a five-paragraph essay on the American Dream. Specifically, he asked if they believed the American Dream was possible for all people in the United States, and to support their arguments with examples and details from their own experiences. The class defined the "American Dream" as having the opportunity, through hard work and good decision making, to have a decent quality of life—to own a home and have a family and enjoy the fruits of your labor.

The English teacher received 92 completed essays from his four sophomore English classes. All told, 57 students believed the American Dream was possible not just for themselves but for everyone, which came to approximately 62 percent of all students. The racial breakdown was as follows: 60 percent of black students thought it was possible (21/35); 62 percent of Latino students thought it was possible (23/37); and 65 percent of whites thought it was possible (13/20). Although the data collection from this essay was far from scientific, the results were interesting enough.

According to the tenets of whiteness studies, one would think a very high percentage of white students, who supposedly lived in a privileged bubble insulated from the reality of race, would assume the American Dream was possible for everyone—simply because it was a reality for them. Likewise, one would think a very low percentage of black and Latino students, who've been oppressed in a systemically racist white supremacist society, would feel the Dream *wasn't* possible.

But this wasn't the case. The belief that a decent quality of life was possible in 2020 was shared nearly equally across the races. The fact that most of these students lived in racially diverse neighborhoods that were comparable in terms of socioeconomics was one reason for the similar responses. Another reason was that these particular kids weren't fixated on race, as they'd grown up in a city that had given them a life's worth of organic cross-racial relationships.

On the flipside, 38 percent of these kids—more than 1 in 3—*didn't* feel the American Dream was possible for everyone. And this too was nearly equal across the races: 40 percent of blacks felt this way (14/35), as did 38 percent of Latinos (14/37), and 35 percent of whites (7/20). These were teenagers, only fourteen or fifteen years old, with their whole lives ahead of them, kids who mostly came from relatively stable homes. Yet instead of dreaming of becoming a doctor or teacher or astronaut, they felt America wasn't really the Land of Opportunity. Their essays articulated their thinking, and although some of their pessimism was based on their own teenage troubles, they used phrases commonly found in antiracist education, loaded words rooted in identity politics.

For example, one student wrote:

> There is such thing as white privilege. It all began during the era of slavery. Whites had everything better than colored people, better bathrooms, schools, water fountains, bus seats, and much more. Nowadays colored people are still treated as the lower class, and whites have a better place in society. They have higher paying jobs and get treated with respect from police officers. They have a way higher advantage in politics and the system for simply being white.

Another student wrote:

> The American Dream is not attainable to me because I am an African American. Being black in today's world doesn't work in my favor. I am constantly racially profiled. I'm seen as angry and I'm supposed to always be strong. How can I achieve the American Dream when I'm one of the most disrespected persons in America?

Still another student said:

> The American Dream isn't really possible for me because I'm African American and a female. Being black and a woman isn't part of the American Dream. . . . People don't even take girls or women seriously because they don't think we are capable. Men are too overpowering, and don't give females a chance to have the American Dream. Women in America are looked down on and are seen as outsiders, and aren't a part of anything.

Tragically, these students were already convinced, before they were even old enough to drive, that America was rigged against them, and that their race or gender was going to disqualify them from being successful and having a good quality of life. And no doubt, this thinking was probably going to negatively affect their grades if it wasn't addressed.

How the differing outlooks on success in America impacted the academic achievement of the English teacher's students was not exactly known, as no real data had been collected to measure this. However, data on standardized tests was available, and from this the English teacher was able to access his own teaching strategies, and how they broke down in terms of racial achievement. During the 2017–2018 school year, because of a gap in Pennsylvania Keystone Exam scores between his school's black students and the rest of the population, the teacher's black students were listed by the Pennsylvania Department of Education as an A-TSI subgroup (Additional Targeted Support and Improvement).

Basically, this meant that over the past year, his school's black students underperformed their peers in algebra and biology, and were a tick below average in literature as well. Being his school's only tenth grade English teacher, he was told at the beginning of the 2018–2019 school year that it was his job to work on raising the overall scores on the Keystone Literature Exam (which were taken at the end of tenth grade), and in particular, the scores of his African American population.

This teacher had been in charge of preparing for the Keystone Literature Exam for nearly a decade, with respectable results, relatively speaking. His school's literature scores were always above the Philadelphia School District average, which wasn't the case for his school's algebra and biology scores, which were consistently below average. And according to the Pennsylvania Value-Added Assessment System (PVAAS), which took into consideration an individual test-taker's past standardized testing history, his students were able to meet most of their projected growth targets in literature.

So as the 2018–2019 school year got underway, the teacher was consistently reminded that he needed to address the gap in scores between his black students and the rest of the population, and that he needed to make sure his teaching wasn't culturally biased in any way. At which point he would ask administrators, "How exactly do you want me to teach our black students differently from the other kids?" There was never a specific answer given, other than the suggested use of more cooperative learning because African American students come from a more collectivist culture than whites.

It was also suggested that he use more culturally responsive teaching, and was given the book, *Culturally Responsive Teaching & The Brain: Promoting Authentic Engagement and Rigor among Culturally and Linguistically Diverse Students*, by Zaretta Hammond, a former English teacher, academic coach, and instructional designer.[22]

The teacher read the book, and realized it was positive and well-meaning, but that it wasn't "a how-to guide on developing culturally responsive lesson plans," nor was it "a prescriptive program outlining how to do culturally responsive teaching," as the author notes in the introduction.[23] The book was more theory and philosophy than methodology, not to the discredit of Ms. Hammond, who did a great job of analyzing the differences between dependent and independent learners, information processing and intellective capacity, and how to bond with students and develop authentic learning partnerships, among many other concepts.

Of course, she also delved into implicit bias, microaggressions, cultural frames of reference, internalized oppression, and stereotype threat, and in the end, the teacher still felt like his original question—*How exactly do you want me to teach our black students differently from the other kids?*—was ultimately left unanswered.

It was at this point that a fellow teacher suggested he visit a website called "#Disrupttexts," which, as mentioned in chapter 4, called on English teachers to dump lesson plans based on universal themes in classic literature, and adopt activities that racialized novels and taught students to view such texts through the lens of racism and white oppression. He went on the site and found a unit titled "Disrupting Shakespeare," which stated:

- We believe in offering students a wide variety of literature and access to playwrights other than Shakespeare. That is valuable, restorative, and productive.
- We believe that Shakespeare, like any other playwright, no more and no less, has literary merit. He is not "universal" in a way that other authors are not. He is not more "timeless" than anyone else.
- We believe he was a man of his time and that his plays harbor problematic depictions and characterizations.[24]

The unit went on to state, "[w]e do not see these same problematic approaches in other plays where whiteness and the male voice are not centered."[25]

The mischaracterization and limited representation of Shakespeare and his work by "#Disrupttexts" was disappointing to the English teacher. Shakespeare's plays and poetry have indeed stood the test of time, as 400 years later he is still performed all over the world to both popular and critical acclaim. His plots, characters, motifs and themes are incredibly complex and wonderfully universal, and have successfully transcended race, religion, gender, and sexuality for centuries. The Bard was clearly a progressive in his day, possibly bisexual, and had the ability to poke fun at the ruling class and bring awareness to social justice issues while still securing the love of the British monarchy.

To appreciate this, of course, takes time and commitment to his work. A superficial and clumsy study of Shakespeare is indeed disastrous, and can no doubt turn a person off to Shakespeare for life. This doesn't mean Shakespeare is archaic and undeserving of special attention, or that his work should be pigeonholed as "white" or "old fashioned." Clearly the team members of "#Disrupttexts" felt differently, as the goal of the group seemed to be educational activism, not appreciation of literature.

Like #Disrupttexts member and English teacher Tricia Ebarvia. Her 2019 blog article, "Disrupting Your Texts: Why Simply Including Diverse Voices Is Not Enough," encouraged teachers to "resist colorblind readings of texts," to "consider the role that race and whiteness have played in your own socialization, particularly around your beliefs about schooling," and to "begin with the premise that public schools never intended to educate all children equally and look for the ways in which this holds true today."[26]

The English teacher took all of this in as he thought of how to raise test scores, coming to realize he wanted to present lessons that were celebratory rather than accusatory. He wanted diversity, sure, but the kind that stemmed from unity and not dichotomy. For him, diverse voices *were* enough, and he realized injecting racial politics into English class wasn't going to make his students better readers, writers, or thinkers. Teens needed to learn cooperation and synergy, as rebellion and resistance were already the default mode of sixteen-year-olds.

That fall the English teacher taught the autobiography *Gifted Hands*, which detailed the incredible achievements of Detroit-native and African American neurosurgeon Dr. Ben Carson, and although it was an easy read, the students understood the themes of hope, goal setting, and the magic of thinking big; they ultimately used this book as a model to write their own autobiographies, which included discussing future aspirations.

He taught the novel *Of Mice and Men*, practicing literary skills and teaching the state standards. He had the students write essays, poems, and constructed responses similar to those on the Keystone Exam. He taught a lesson on author's technique, and how the use of characterization affected the theme of loneness and isolation.

And although he briefly touched on the issue of segregation when discussing the African American character of Crooks, he ultimately used a colorblind approach, focusing on the universal human emotions that unified the characters and made them the same—how Crooks, and Candy, and Lennie, and Curley, were all just suffering human beings at their core, lonely, misunderstood, and unable to communicate effectively, simply living day-to-day and trying to survive the Great Depression.

And it was clear that at the height of the novel, when the power of Steinbeck's words worked their magic, every student in the teacher's class, no matter their race or gender or sexuality, could identify with one of those characters, because who hasn't felt lonely, or rejected, or misunderstood in their lifetime? Who hasn't felt the cold isolation of not having a friend? And they engaged in the lesson fully, and the English teacher treated them equally, and they learned.

That spring the English teacher did Shakespeare's *Othello*, despite the advice of #Disrupttexts. And although he briefly touched on the discrimination Othello faced at the hands of the smug Venetians—who thought they were God's gift to sixteenth-century Europe—he chose a colorblind approach with this story as well, not harping on racism and privilege but instead highlighting the universal human emotions that made Shakespeare's work so powerful, so wise, so artistic and timeless, like the destructive nature of jealousy, and how this emotion managed to take down the best of characters despite the best of intentions, and how this feeling didn't stop to consider race, or gender, or sexuality.

And at the height of the play, when Othello realizes he's killed the love of his life despite the fact she was the most loyal companion a man could ever want, and he breaks down and cries over his fatal mistake, and his students sat on the edges of their seats, black as well as white, hanging on every Shakespearean word, he knew the unit had worked. He believed in the material, and he believed in them. Equally. And it worked.

In May, two months after *Othello* and seven months after *Gifted Hands* and *Of Mice and Men*, his students took the 2019 Keystone Literature Exam. Not only did his students meet their PVAAS growth targets, but his African American students made up the skills gap as well. As a subgroup, 48 percent passed the exam, which was not only 5 percent higher than the school average (all students), but was also 12 percent higher than the district average (all students), and 1 percent higher than the Pennsylvania state average (all students).[27]

He was proud of them to say the least.

RECOMMENDATIONS

1. Preservice teachers need more hands-on instructional methods that include culturally responsive teaching, and less strategies that focus on the perceived problems of whiteness. In short, they need skills-based approaches to develop democratic classrooms that welcome all voices, not politics-based ones.

2. Studies show that students of color receive less rigorous assignments and lessons than their white counterparts, and score lower on standardized tests. This could be the result of stereotype threat, and the fact that a hyperfocus on race and racism is creating a "threat in the air." The possibility that whiteness studies is having a negative effect on teacher expectations—that it's perpetuating a cycle it's ironically trying to end—is an idea that must be further investigated and explored.

3. A celebratory approach to diversity in schools, which positively highlights cultural differences and racial unity, is more appropriate than an accusatory antiracist approach, which is zero-sum and dualistic in nature.

NOTES

1. Megan E. Lynch, "The Hidden Nature of Whiteness in Education: Creating Active Allies in White Teachers," *Journal of Educational Supervision*, Vol. 1, No. 1 (2018), 18–31.
2. Ibid., 18.
3. Ibid., 22.
4. Lauren Camera, "U.S. Students Show No Improvement in Math, Reading, Science on International Exam," *US News & World Report*, December 3, 2019, https://www.usnews.com (accessed January 25, 2020).
5. Paul E. Barton and Richard J. Coley, *The Black-White Achievement Gap: When Progress Stopped* (Princeton, NJ: Educational Test Service, July, 2010), https://www.ets.org (accessed January 29, 2020), 3.
6. Peggy McIntosh, "White Privilege: Unpacking the Invisible Knapsack," *Peace and Freedom Magazine*, July/August, 1989, 10–12.

7. Robert Rosenthal and Lenore Jacobson, *Pygmalion in the Classroom: Teacher Expectation and Pupils' Intellectual Development*, (New York: Holt, Rinehart and Winston, 1968).

8. Robin DiAngelo, *What Does It Mean to Be White?: Developing White Cultural Literacy Revised* (New York: Peter Lang, 2016).

9. Ibid.

10. "The Opportunity Myth," The New Teacher Project, 2018, https://tntp.org (accessed February 21, 2020), 6.

11. Ibid., 45.

12. Carrie Barron, "When Not Talking about Past Trauma Is Wise," *Psychology Today*, January 27, 2015, https://www.psychologytoday.com (accessed February 24, 2020).

13. Zaretta Hammond, *Culturally Responsive Teaching & the Brain: Promoting Authentic Engagement and Rigor Among Culturally and Linguistically Diverse Students* (Thousand Oaks, California: Corwin, 2015), 32–33.

14. Steve Stroessner and Catherine Good, "Stereotype Threat: An Overview," *Reducing Stereotype Threat*, http://www.reducingstereotypethreat.org/ (accessed December 3, 2019).

15. "Stereotype Threat Widens Achievement Gap," *American Psychological Association*, July 15, 2006, https://www.apa.org (accessed November 30, 2019).

16. Jonathan Church, "Lee Jussim Is Right to Be Skeptical about 'Stereotype Threat'," *Quillette*, February 22, 2020, https://www.quillette.com (accessed February 24, 2020).

17. Ibid.

18. Robin DiAngelo, *What Does It Mean to Be White?: Developing White Cultural Literacy Revised* (New York: Peter Lang, 2016), 76–77.

19. Steven J. Spencer, Christine Logel, and Paul G. Davies, "Stereotype Threat," *Annual Review of Psychology*, Vol. 67 (2016), 415–437.

20. Ibid., 428.

21. Ibid.

22. Zaretta Hammond, *Culturally Responsive Teaching & the Brain*.

23. Ibid., p. 5.

24. #Disrupttexts, "Disrupting Shakespeare," October 25, 2018, https://disrupttexts.org (accessed February 26, 2020).

25. Ibid.

26. Tricia Ebarvia, "Disrupting Your Texts: Why Simply Including Diverse Voices Is Not Enough," International Literacy Association, September 5, 2019, https://www.literacyworldwide.org (accessed January 26, 2020).

27. Pennsylvania Keystone Exams, 2019 English Keystone Summary Report, Swenson Arts and Technology HS, Philadelphia City SD, Spring 2019.

Chapter Nine

Solutions

Diversity Through Unity

In his fifth edition of *Cultural Diversity and Education,* research scholar and "father" of multicultural education, James A. Banks, offers an interesting approach to fair and equitable education called *multicultural ideology.* Published in 2006, it's less aggressive and confrontational than current 2020 antiracist educational approaches, which tend to be more accusatory than celebratory; in 2006, mainstream multicultural education focused on unity over dichotomy, which is no longer the case today, as zero-sum antiracist philosophies—which seek to dismantle so-called problematic "whiteness"—are now heavily influencing policies and perspectives.

Multicultural ideology is a blending of educational concepts by assimilationists and cultural pluralists. Assimilationists feel all Americans should conform to a traditional national identity, one not sensitive to the diversity of America in the twenty-first century. In other words, an America based not only on the values and principles that made the United States one of the richest and most technologically advanced countries in the world—like freedom, liberty, individualism, and entrepreneurship—but also on white, male, Judeo-Christian values and customs.

An assimilationist approach suggests that to end suffering and disenfranchisement, all immigrants and people of color must assimilate to this "white" traditional identity in order to gain equality and full access to resources. This ideology is often critiqued as racist in that it believes in, and publicly calls for, a white dominant culture at the expense of racial minorities.

According to Banks:

> Not only do assimilationists view ethnicity as inconsistent with modernized societies, they believe that strong ethnic attachments are dysfunctional in a modernized civic community. . . . The assimilationist sees integration as a societal goal in a modernized state, not ethnic segregation or separation. The assimilationist thinks that the best way to promote the goals of society and to develop commitments to democratic ideals is to promote the full socialization of all individuals and groups into the shared national civic culture.[1]

Cultural pluralists are the opposite extreme of assimilationists, and believe the key to strength and equality not only requires complete and total diversity, but also the fundamental dismantling of the white establishment and the remaking of America itself. In other words, everything is illegitimate and must go: the oppressive white, male, Judeo-Christian values and customs, *as well as* traditional American ideals—such as capitalism, individualism, and meritocracy—which stem from the dominant white culture and are therefore oppressive by default.

This approach can be seen as a counter-offensive against classic assimilation, a deconstruction of the "white" national identity which perpetuates white supremacy and fosters racial inequality. In short, capitalism is replaced with socialism; individualism is replaced with collectivism; meritocracy is replaced with social justice.

According to Banks:

> It is extremely important, argues the pluralist, for individuals to develop a commitment to their cultures and ethnic group, especially if that group is oppressed by more powerful groups within society. The energies and skills of each member of a culture or ethnic group are needed to help in that group's liberation struggle. Each member of the group has a moral obligation to join the liberation struggle. Thus, the pluralist stresses the rights of the group over the rights of the individual.[2]

In the twenty-first century, the pluralists have redefined themselves as social justice activists and operate under an "antiracist" framework, where biological race doesn't exist but its social construct does; where institutional patterns take precedent over personal values; where "whiteness" is inherently racist and always rewarded; where "color" is inherently free of racism and eternally oppressed.

Where colorblindness, being a denial of "privilege," is frowned upon; where a hyperfocus on race, being an affirmation of social change, is applauded; where microaggressions and unconscious biases dictate behavior; where a white person's intentions are rendered meaningless if they are perceived as racist by a person of color; and where America is viewed as illegitimate, being that its founders were murderers and thieves.

The third approach, which reflects the first two positions yet avoids their extremes, is *multicultural ideology*. This is a blending of assimilation and cultural pluralism, where the American national identity adapts and develops to become more diverse and pluralistic, yet doesn't abandon the nation's core values—the fundamental principles that make America unique and one of the most successful countries in the world. In *Cultural Diversity and Education*, Banks writes that multicultural ideology is reflected in educational policy that is "guided by an eclectic ideology that reflects both the cultural pluralist position and the assimilation position, but avoids their extremes."[3]

Though Banks calls multicultural ideology an "ideal-type concept"—which means it does not define any specific case, nor does it accurately describe the views of any particular writer or theorist—it can still serve as a guidepost for a holistic solution to inequality in America. It's an ideology that doesn't view individualism, meritocracy, entrepreneurship, or the free market as tools of the dominant culture, but as a set of building blocks that anyone can use to achieve success.

It operates under the premise that although there are systemic and historical injustices that must be adequately addressed and rectified, the American Dream isn't "white," and that a universal set of American ideals can be applied across all races, religions, genders, and sexualities.

In twenty-first-century America, the cultural war is being primarily fought between the multicultural ideologists and the cultural pluralists, although the pluralists have managed to frame the war as assimilation vs. pluralism. The pluralists have also successfully co-opted pop culture language and managed to redefine terms like "racism," "white supremacy," "colorblindness," and "individualism" to reflect definitions aligned with the goals of antiracism. Still, the pluralists are not just fighting for equality; they're fighting to fundamentally transform and remake America, culturally and economically. They believe America is illegitimate, founded on genocide and theft and built on slavery and oppression.

Although slavery and oppression are a legitimate part of America's history, so are its founding principles of freedom, liberty, individualism, and the right to limited government—all of which have made America one of the greatest countries in the world, a beacon light of hope for the tens of thousands of immigrants who flock to the United States every year from all over the globe.

As noted previously, much of DiAngelo's work is driven by the central question, "What does it mean to be white in a society that proclaims race meaningless, yet is deeply divided by race?"[4] Yet this statement is disingenuous, as it claims society thinks race *doesn't* matter. A more accurate view held by Americans, as documented earlier in this book, it's that they think it *shouldn't* matter.

When white Americans call for universalism and speak of treating people of color simply as fellow human beings, they mean skin color *shouldn't* make a difference. Granted, people of color are made aware of their race more often than whites, and some whites do live in a segregated bubble where they may not think race makes a difference in their lives; Robin DiAngelo freely admits growing up in such a bubble.[5]

But the core premise of traditional colorblindness is that society shouldn't use race to judge character, or to profile, or to punish, or as a means to grant access to resources. Likewise, universal human qualities such as love, compassion, respect, tolerance, and trust *are* free from race, and can serve as a guidepost for healing racial divisions and promoting equality and access to America's resources, and can help teachers bond and connect with their students in order to better educate them.

There's an interesting irony among traditional white educators who believe in universality, and whiteness scholars who do not: traditional educators hope to end racism by filtering out skin color and interacting with people through fundamental human values, both at the conscious and subconscious levels; whiteness scholars hope to end racism by becoming hyperfocused on race and the cerebral concepts of implicit bias and microaggressions in order to end so-called white supremacy culture.

The former creates a society based on values from the heart, where both racism and the preoccupation with skin color are gone for good. The latter creates a world where, in theory, racism ends through an intellectual process which analyzes and rejects all forms of bias whether conscious or unconscious, but still leaves us with a hyperfocus on race.

Using race to end racism is similar to the approach Hindus and Buddhists use to reach enlightenment: you use your mind to transcend your mind. Or, as revered Indian spiritual teacher Ranjit Maharaj once taught: you use a thorn to remove a thorn, then throw them both away.[6] But the problem with a whiteness scholar's approach is that you use race to remove racism, but you don't throw them both away: you *heighten* race and intensify its focus.

This is perhaps done by design. By redefining "racism" to mean inherent white privilege and oppression, all whites become guilty by default. Thus "whiteness" becomes "racism," which ultimately transforms the property of whiteness into the commodity of racism, and enables the politically oriented whiteness studies movement to usurp whiteness to use and redistribute as it sees fit.

Which is why, after whiteness scholars use race to get rid of racism, they don't throw them both away. For folks like DiAngelo, race is too powerful to ever let go of. It's too easy to use as a cudgel to wield over those who refuse to espouse the identity politics at the heart of antiracism. In a strange way, antiracism has become what it's fighting against, in that it views the world and all its people through the lens of skin color.

Whether intentional or not, antiracism goes against the teachings of Freire in that the oppressed don't liberate themselves *and* their oppressor; because it is zero-sum, antiracism invalidates the supposed oppressor, delegitimizes them, discredits them, and aims to fundamentally transform them into something completely different. This isn't liberation; this is *transformation*. It's revolution, and not at all compassionate or unifying. It's not a coexistence, in that it requires the complete reinvention of the supposed oppressor's culture, value system, and heritage, "niceness" be damned.

DiAngelo and her fellow whiteness scholars aim to replace capitalism with socialism, individualism with collectivism, and meritocracy with "social justice." They believe America is an illegitimate country founded by murderers and thieves, and are fighting to finally make things right. As DiAngelo states in the acknowledgments section of *What Does iI Mean to Be White?*, the "theft of Indigenous lands was the starting point of our current racial system."[7]

But this zero-sum approach—believing that the disruption and transformation of one group is needed for the advancement of another—is misguided and limited. There indeed exists a universal system of shared human values that make it possible for all Americans to have equal access to resources, values that transcend race and do not depend on the divisive politics of identity. To tap into these resources, however, one must forfeit both ego and politics, and get out of their mind and open their heart.

LEAVING THE MIND AND ENTERING THE HEART

In Zen Buddhism, the word "prajna" is used to describe the wisdom of having a direct insight into truth. Put another way, it's the ability to see the true nature of phenomena, which is infinite and empty of any inherent limitations. The limitations we do see stem from our small finite minds, which serve as a prism through which we view universal Consciousness or Big Mind (also known as Buddha Nature).

In effect, all of our small finite minds co-create reality together, using our past experiences to shape our judgments and form our perspectives. But those who develop prajna wisdom begin to see a bigger picture of reality, and start to understand that there is no inherent separateness in anything; a teacup can only hold tea because of the form (the cup itself) and emptiness (the space inside). Thus form is emptiness and emptiness is form, and not only do both depend on each other for their existence, but there is no real dividing line between the two. For what is the essence of "teacup-ness"? If one were to take a teacup apart, at what point would the teacup cease being a teacup?

One way Zen practitioners develop prajna wisdom is through meditation, which is simply sitting still in one position and allowing the mind to settle by focusing on the breath. This is incredibly difficult, as the human mind is usually filled with excessive chatter, and has a tendency to jump from one thought to the next. The trick is to stay present by paying attention to the behavior of the mind, and to refocus it on the breath when it starts to wander. After several days or a week of regular meditation, a Zen practitioner will start to notice their mind slightly settling down.

If a person sticks with it for months or even years, the mind will quiet to the point where they can begin to live their life with what is called "effortless effort," which means they are present enough to allow right actions to arise by themselves, without a lot of tedious thinking and mental chatter. In other words, they are so attuned to the present moment (and so free of mental noise) that the clarity of their mind allows them to have direct insight into truth—which is nothing more than an intuitive and instinctive understanding of what is the right choice of action at any given moment.

Another term for this is "being in the zone." The world's greatest musicians, artists, and athletes have all done their best work in this zone, when they learned how to get out of their own way and simply allow things to flow. Of course, this "flow" can get interrupted at any moment. Self-doubt arises, or the hot baseball player—who's on a ten-game hitting streak—suddenly becomes self-conscious of the mechanics of his swing and *bang*, the streak ends as quickly as it began. The gut feeling, or instinct, is gone. In the world of art, the muse disappears. Where did it go? Who knows. But often times, the artist or athlete is left stuck in their own head, trying to use their mind to reason their way out.

Whiteness studies, and the approaches at the heart of antiracism, are very cerebral in nature. Interestingly, they do not quiet the mind, but do the exact opposite: they stimulate an abundance of intellectual processing, creating endless streams of mental analysis throughout the course of daily life, often agitating the mind; when whites complain that antiracist work is difficult or uncomfortable, they're most likely referring to the mental agitation and neurosis that develops.

Because whiteness studies teaches that all white people have implicit biases and microaggressions, whites are required to constantly monitor and unpack their beliefs, motives, intentions, and so forth, in an effort to scrub them free of racism. In other words, they are being taught to become self-conscious of the mechanics of their swing. And not just for one game, but *for their whole career*. Remember, whites who evolve to the highest stage of WRID enthusiastically embrace their lifelong role as social and political activists fighting against the injustice of white supremacy, pledging to keep the politics of race and racism at the forefront of their lives, continuously monitoring their own unconscious biases and microaggressions.[8]

There are a number of side effects of such a cerebral existence. For starters, it increases mental noise, and can cause paralysis by analysis. Worse still, it may lead to the condescension or patronization of people of color. Last year a friend from college—who was in Philadelphia for a social work conference—was in the grocery store buying some things for her weekend stay. Although she was from an all-white suburb of Boston, she was very progressive and prided herself on being "woke."

A black man started ringing up her purchases, and instead of taking a colorblind approach and treating this person like any other person, she started to monitor her own thinking and behavior: *Should I bag the groceries myself, or let the black cashier do it? If I let him do it, he might think I'm racist, that I'm too good to bag the groceries because of white privilege. This could be a microaggression, and I don't want to offend him. But what if I bag the groceries myself, and the black cashier mistakenly thinks I'm racist because I don't feel he is capable of doing it right because he's black?*

Inevitably, the thoughts that went through her head reflected in her body language, and she came off exactly as she intended not to: as a patronizing white woman who was unable to look past race and simply treat this person as a person. She confirmed these very thoughts later in a conversation over dinner, after she had a few drinks. When she asked advice on the matter, a friend told her not to think in terms of color. Instead, the friend suggested she should have simply treated this person as a person, using the universal value of teamwork and cooperation to bag the groceries with him from the start, coming from her heart instead of her head.

Examples like these are not isolated cases in grocery stores in Philadelphia. Young white teachers are being taught to be overly cerebral when it comes to race in America's classrooms, and struggle when it comes to disciplining students of color. At the start of the 2019–2020 school year in New York City, rookie educators were given an essay to read titled "Dear White Teacher," which addressed this very issue. According to the *New York Post*, "Essay author Chrysanthius Lathan blasts white teachers who she says routinely send minority students to 'teachers of color' for discipline—because they're scared of being called racist."[9]

The overly cerebral nature of whiteness studies and identity politics can also cause teachers to become rigid, and make their behavior come off as contrived. How loose and spontaneous can an educator be when they are constantly checking their privilege, monitoring racial bias, and focusing their attention on the race, religion, gender, and sexuality of the student they are interacting with? New teachers are already nervous and overwhelmed, without having to psychoanalyze themselves for hidden bigotry.

It's not uncommon for white rookie educators teaching in Philadelphia to become immobilized by a preoccupation with the identity of their students, and they all look the same: tight, mechanical, and humorless. They walk on P.C. eggshells and can't bond or connect with anyone. Again, a freer and much more liberating approach would be if they dropped out of their minds and into their hearts, and simply interacted with their students as *people*, being proactive instead of reactive, using universal means of communication such as active listening, and readily employing patience, trust, compassion, and love.

These transcend race, religion, gender, and sexuality, and do not involve rigid intellectual processes that agitate the mind and hinder spontaneity and flow. This keeps an educator grounded in the present, and allows them to focus on the immediacy of the situation at hand, without adding any extra mental "story" to things. As spiritual teacher Eckhart Tolle writes, it's the "power of now." Educators who come from the heart are open and genuine, and their students notice this and respond positively. And when teachers effectively bond with their students, any unconscious mental biases usually dissolve on their own.

THE MAGIC OF UNITY

The double standards at the heart of whiteness studies and antiracism are many. Tragically, the fact that there are one set of rules for whites, and another set of rules for people of color does a disservice to the very cause of antiracism—which is to level the playing field and bring people of all races equal access to America's resources. Believing that "whiteness" is a fundamental problem that must be solved is not the best approach to opening the minds of whites. Likewise, embracing anti-whiteness is no real way to stop anti-blackness, although whiteness scholars like DiAngelo seem to believe otherwise.

In her best seller *White Fragility*, DiAngelo dedicates an entire chapter to "Anti-Blackness," where she states that "in the white mind, black people are the ultimate racial 'other,'" and even says that she herself recognizes "the deep anti-black feelings" that have been inculcated in her since childhood.[10] She writes, "[t]hese feelings surface immediately—in fact, before I can even think—when I conceptualize black people in general," and insists that "anti-blackness is foundational to our very identities as white people."[11] She goes on to write:

> Whiteness has always been predicated on blackness. . . . there was no concept of race or a white race before the need to justify the enslavement of Africans. Creating a separate and inferior black race simultaneously created the "superior" white race: one concept could not exist without the other.[12]

Her belief in such a notion is the very definition of zero-sum: what is gained by one side is lost by the other. "To put it bluntly," she writes, "I believe that the white collective fundamentally hates blackness for what it reminds us of: that we are capable and guilty of perpetuating immeasurable harm and that our gains come through the subjugation of others."[13]

Her words are concerning for a number of reasons. First, they give us a window into her own psyche—how her life experiences and environment conditioned her to view people and the world around her. It's an unfortunate view, to say the least. Granted, she's addressing society at the macro-level and doesn't harbor any resentment to anyone personally—as she has black friends whom she "loves deeply"—but her unconscious feelings about the black collective are troubling.

This kind of outlook on the world is questionable, as there's no hard data to specifically prove America's anti-blackness. Saying so, of course, runs counter to the principles of whiteness studies, and as such, is evidence of white fragility; in an ironic way, it's almost as if whites are being *coerced* by whiteness scholars into accepting their "anti-blackness," even if it means they must will it into existence.

Second, and more importantly, DiAngelo's concept of anti-blackness exhibits a familiar double standard: it offers a different set of rules for whites and people of color. Specifically, anti-blackness is criticized for the fact that it's zero-sum—that white superiority depends on the creation of black inferiority. Yet the supposed solution at the heart of whiteness studies commits the same transgression: that people of color must be uplifted through *anti-whiteness*, or by the dismantling or decentering of whiteness.

It's well documented by DiAngelo herself that whiteness studies have an adverse effect on white people. In much of her writing, she describes the negative reactions of whites in anti-bias trainings, graduate classes, and in other situations—all of which are diagnosed as examples of white fragility. The fact that these antiracist approaches, despite eliciting such adverse reactions, continue to be put upon whites is reminiscent of a concept made popular by Dr. David R. Hawkins called "Power vs. Force," which analyzes "the hidden determinants of human behavior."[14]

While true power resides from within, force is applied through projection—an outside force trying to impose its will. Force can only work for so long; once it encounters true power, it immediately unravels. Interestingly, many of the emotions cited by DiAngelo as evidence of white fragility—such as anger, shame, guilt, and apathy—are listed by Hawkins as being a reaction to force. Nowhere in white fragility theory or whiteness studies can one find positive responses related to true power, such as courage, love, joy, or enlightenment; everything tied to white fragility is zero-sum and is based on dichotomy rather than unity.

But for some reason, unity—as well as universalism, colorblindness, and other concepts which prioritize racial harmony over dichotomy—are resisted by whiteness scholars. Such things are delegitimized and even stigmatized, and often rebranded by antiracists as *perpetuating* racism.

This is necessary in part to shock sheltered whites out of their bubbles and bring systemic racism to light, but whiteness scholars take it a step further:

they highlight it to increase the power and reach of identity politics. But the simple fact is that America needs more racial unity, and less confrontation. Provoking whites, and agitating their psyches with the notion that they all suffer from implicit bias and are perpetuating racism by default, is limited in its effectiveness.

The goal of disturbing a white person's racial comfort in order to disrupt a supposed racial hierarchy is too radical an approach to make any meaningful progress in terms of equity and race relations. Whites may be pressured into compliance, but is this compliance genuine and long lasting? And is this compliance ultimately empowering people of color to live independently from the crutch of identity politics? More research must be done to answer these important questions.

As evidenced by the election of Barack Obama, many whites in America are open-minded, caring, and want racial equality. In short, they are ready and willing to help those who are underserved, underrepresented, and need an extra hand. But unfortunately, instead of framing inequality as a problem that must be solved through whites and people of color working together and meeting halfway, antiracists hold whites solely responsible, while absolving people of color of all accountability. This is a recipe for failure and resentment.

Take affirmative action, for example. Imagine if proponents of racial quotas framed the issue this way: *people of color are struggling for a multitude of reasons, so please, white brothers and sisters, lend them a hand because they need that extra push. Yes, you have been part of the problem, but we need to work together.* If this were the message, not only would most whites gladly get on board, but also those who didn't would be hard-pressed to find a reasonable counterargument.

But unfortunately, when it comes to affirmative action, this isn't the message. Like the core tenets behind whiteness studies, the message is more like this: *people of color are owed preferential treatment, because racist whites—who have an unearned privilege—have been oppressing them for centuries.* Is this really the best way to elicit the help of "white allies"? To accuse caring and open-minded people, who were not even alive during slavery and segregation, of perpetuating systemic racism?

Common sense would say it's not. But imagine if the arrogant, accusatory tone of whiteness scholars was replaced with a more genuine request for help? *Hey, white people, can you lend your colored brothers and sisters a hand? The world is a difficult place, and no one willfully intends to live in poverty, so how about taking inventory of the situation and giving those folks who may be struggling a place in line? In fact, why not do something totally out of the box and give them YOUR place in line, just for today? After all, you are also responsible for this situation.*

Imagine if all the "anti" approaches, like those at the heart of antiracism and anti-bias, became "pro" approaches, and shifted from an accusatory tone of privilege and oppression to one of celebration and unity? Instead of dividing people into affinity groups by race, and religion, and gender, and sexuality, why not mix folks together and ask them to analyze *how they are the same?* How suffering is suffering, no matter the color of your skin? How joy is joy, no matter the pronoun you use? How it hurts to be lied to and cheated on, and how grief can cut you down and blow your world to bits?

Imagine if people were given such trainings? Imagine if whites weren't told that they were perpetuating racism by default, and blacks weren't told that they were being eternally victimized, and both groups weren't divided into dualistic camps and fed the notion that one group's gain was the other group's loss, and instead were reminded of the Golden Rule: *do unto others as you'd have them do unto you*?

This wouldn't be good for identity politics, sure, but it just might bring some real progress in a world desperately in need of unity, communication, understanding, and love.

RECOMMENDATIONS

1. Multicultural education, which uses a *multicultural ideology* based on unity rather than dichotomy, should be incorporated in America's schools. This is a blending of assimilation and cultural pluralism, where the American national identity adapts and develops to become more diverse and pluralistic, yet doesn't abandon the nation's core values—the fundamental principles that make America unique and one of the most successful countries in the world.

2. "Anti" approaches, like those at the heart of antiracism and anti-bias, should become "pro" approaches, and shift from an accusatory tone of privilege and oppression to one of celebration and unity. Instead of dividing people into affinity groups by race, and religion, and gender, and sexuality, professors should mix preservice teachers together and ask them to analyze *how they are the same?*

3. New teachers should stay focused in the present moment, and not get caught up in the "chatter mind" of identity politics. They should drop out of their heads and into their hearts, and simply interact with their students as *people*, being proactive instead of reactive, using universal means of communication such as active listening, and readily employing patience, trust, compassion, and love.

NOTES

1. James A. Banks, *Cultural Diversity and Education: Foundations, Curriculum, and Teaching, Fifth Edition* (Boston, MA: Pearson Education, Inc., 2006), 115.
2. Ibid., 116.
3. Ibid., 117
4. Robin DiAngelo, *What Does It Mean to Be White?: Developing White Cultural Literacy Revised* (New York: Peter Lang, 2016), 14.
5. Robin DiAngelo, *What Does It Mean to Be White?*, 175–160.
6. Ranjit Maharaj, *Illusion vs. Reality* (Sadguru Publishing, 2010), 6.
7. Robin DiAngelo, *What Does It Mean to Be White?*, x.
8. Joseph G. Ponterotto, Shawn O. Utsey, and Paul B. Pedersen, *Preventing Prejudice* (Thousand Oaks, CA: Sage Publications, 2006), 88–108.
9. Carl Campanile, Selim Algar and Bruce Golding, "New NYC Teachers Given Book with Essay Titled 'Dear White Teacher'," *New York Post*, September 3, 2019, https://nypost.com (access March 8, 2020).
10. Robin DiAngelo, *White Fragility: Why It's So Hard for White People to Talk about Racism* (Boston: Beacon Press, 2018), 94–105.
11. Ibid.
12. Ibid.
13. Ibid.
14. David R. Hawkins, *Power vs. Force: The Hidden Determinants of Human Behavior* (West Sedona, AZ: Veritas Publishing, 2013).

Bibliography

Action News, 6ABC Philadelphia. "Commissioner: Philadelphia Officer Did Not Want to Make Starbucks Arrest." April 16, 2018. Accessed December 31, 2019. https://6abc.com.

Algar, Selim. "DOE-Sponsored Group Said Asians Benefit from White Privilege: Parent." *New York Post*, May 26, 2019. https://nypost.com.

American Psychological Association. "Stereotype Threat Widens Achievement Gap." July 15, 2006. Accessed March 18, 2020. https://www.apa.org.

Anderson, Monica, Mark Hugo Lopez, and Molly Rohal. "A Rising Share of the U.S. Black Population Is Foreign Born." Pew Research Center, April 9, 2015. https://www.pewsocialtrends.org.

Arnesen, Eric. "Whiteness and the Historians' Imagination." *International Labor and Working-Class History* 60 (Fall 2001): 3–32.

Association of Delaware Valley Independent Schools, "MCRC@ADVIS Critical Conversations." March 12, 2020. Accessed March 16, 2020. https://www.advis.org/default.aspx?relID=756017595.

Banks, James A. *Cultural Diversity and Education: Foundations, Curriculum, and Teaching, Fifth Edition*. Boston, MA: Pearson Education, Inc., 2006.

Barr, Andy. "Holder: 'Nation of Cowards' on Race." *Politico*, February 18, 2009. https://www.politico.com.

Barron, Carrie. "When Not Talking about Past Trauma Is Wise." *Psychology Today*, January 27, 2015. https://www.psychologytoday.com.

Barton, Paul E. and Richard J. Coley. *Parsing the Achievement Gap II*. Princeton, NJ: Educational Test Service, April, 2009. https://www.ets.org/Media/Research/pdf/PICPARSINGII.pdf.

Barton, Paul E. and Richard J. Coley. *The Black-White Achievement Gap: When Progress Stopped*. Princeton, NJ: Educational Test Service, July, 2010. https://origin-www.ets.org/Media/Research/pdf/PICBWGAP.pdf.

Barton, Paul E. and Richard J. Coley. *The Family: America's Smallest School*. Princeton, NJ: Educational Test Service, September, 2007. https://www.ets.org/Media/Education_Topics/pdf/5678_PERCReport_School.pdf.

Bennett, Jacob. "White Privilege: A History of the Concept." Master's Thesis, Georgia State University Department of History, April 11, 2012. https://scholarworks.gsu.edu.

Calefati, Jessica, Dylan Purcell and Kristen A. Graham. "Turnstile Teaching." *Philadelphia Inquirer*, April 26, 2019. https://www.inquirer.com.

Camera, Lauren. "U.S. Students Show No Improvement in Math, Reading, Science on International Exam." *US News & World Report*, December 3, 2019. https://www.usnews.com.

Campanile, Carl, Selim Algar and Bruce Golding. "New NYC Teachers Given Book with Essay Titled 'Dear White Teacher'." *New York Post*, September 3, 2019. https://nypost.com.

Castagno, Angelina E. *The Price of Nice: How Good Intentions Maintain Educational Inequity*. Minneapolis: University of Minnesota Press, 2019.

CBS New York. "Lawyer for Women Suing Dept. of Education Speaks Out." May 30, 2019. Accessed February 29, 2020. https://newyork.cbslocal.com.

Chang, David. "Philly Chess Team Wins Back-to-Back National Titles." NBC10 Philadelphia, April 30, 2014. Accessed February 2, 2020. https://www.nbcphiladelphia.com.

Church, Jonathan. "Lee Jussim Is Right to Be Skeptical about 'Stereotype Threat'." *Quillette*, February 22, 2020. https://www.quillette.com.

Church, Jonathan. "The Epistemological Problem of White Fragility Theory." *Areo*, December 21, 2018. https://areomagazine.com.

Church, Jonathan. "The Problem I Have with the Concept of White Privilege." *The Good Men Project*, March 19, 2017. https://goodmenproject.com.

Church, Jonathan. "The Theory of White Fragility: Scholarship or Proselytization?" *Areo*, January 25, 2019. https://areomagazine.com.

Church, Jonathan. "Whiteness Studies: An Insidious Ideology." *The Agonist*, July 1, 2019. http://theagonist.org.

Church, Jonathan. "Whiteness Studies and the Theory of White Fragility Are Based on a Logical Fallacy." *Areo*, April 25, 2019. https://areomagazine.com.

Collins, Cory. "What Is White Privilege, Really?" *Teaching Tolerance* 60 (Fall 2018). https://www.tolerance.org.

Crenshaw, Kimberle. "Demarginalizing the Intersection of Race and Sex: A Black Feminist Critique of Antidiscrimination Doctrine, Feminist Theory and Antiracist Politics." *University of Chicago Legal Forum* 1989, no. 1 (1989).

DiAngelo, Robin, Ali Michael and Toni Graves Williamson. "ADVIS Critical Conversations: White Fragility and Affinity Group Webinar." Association of Delaware Valley Independent Schools, March 12, 2020.

DiAngelo, Robin. *What Does It Mean to Be White?: Developing White Cultural Literacy Revised*. New York: Peter Lang, 2016.

DiAngelo, Robin. "White Fragility." *The International Journal of Critical Pedagogy* 3, no. 3 (2011). http://libjournal.uncg.edu.

DiAngelo, Robin. *White Fragility: Why It's So Hard for White People to Talk about Racism*. Boston: Beacon Press, 2018.

Disrupttexts. "Disrupting Shakespeare." October 25, 2018. Accessed March 18, 2020. https://disrupttexts.org.

Dobbin, Frank and Alexandra Kalev. "Why Diversity Programs Fail." *Harvard Business Review*, July–August, 2016. https://hbr.org.

Ebarvia, Tricia. "Disrupting Your Texts: Why Simply Including Diverse Voices Is Not Enough." International Literacy Association, September 5, 2019. https://www.literacyworldwide.org.

Edelman, Susan. "Schools Chancellor Richard Carranza Accused of Demoting Admins because They Were White." *New York Post*, May 18, 2019. https://nypost.com.

Edelman, Susan. "Teachers Allegedly Told to Favor Black Students in 'Racial Equity' Training." *New York Post*, May 25, 2019. https://nypost.com.

Edelman, Susan and Selim Algar. "Fourth White DOE Executive Sues over Racial Discrimination." *New York Post*, October 1, 2019. https://nypost.com.

Edelman, Susan, Selim Algar and Aaron Feis. "Richard Carranza Held 'White-Supremacy Culture' Training for School Admins." *New York Post*, May 20, 2019. https://nypost.com.

Elder, Larry. "The Meaning of Charleston." *Townhall*, June 25, 2015. https://townhall.com.

Elliott, Kathleen. "Challenging Toxic Masculinity in Schools and Society." *On the Horizon* 26, no. 1 (2018): 17–22.

Fontenot, Kayla, Jessica Semega, and Melissa Kollar. "Income and Poverty in the United States: 2017." United States Census Bureau, September 2018. Accessed January 23, 2020. https://www.census.gov.

Freire, Paulo. *Pedagogy of the Oppressed, 30th Anniversary edition.* New York: Continuum, 2000.
Fry, Madeline. "In Seattle, Math Is Cultural Appropriation." *Washington Examiner*, October 23, 2019. https://www.washingtonexaminer.com.
Garcia, Melissa. "Why Teachers Must Fight Their Own Implicit Biases." *Education Week*, July 25, 2018. https://www.edweek.org.
Goodwin, Michael. "Richard Carranza's Prejudicial Race Politics Have Gone Too Far." *New York Post*, May 28, 2019. https://nypost.com.
Graham, Kristen A. "How Philly Schools Are Cutting Out Bad Behavior and Improving Academics." *Philadelphia Inquirer*, February 16, 2018. https://www.inquirer.com.
Griffith, David and Adam Tyner. *Discipline Reform through the Eyes of Teachers.* Washington, DC: Thomas B. Fordham Institute (July 30, 2019). http://fordhaminstitute.org/national/research/ discipline-reform-through-the-eyes-of-teachers.
Halle, Tamara. "Charting Parenthood: A Statistical Portrait of Fathers and Mothers in America." Child Trends, 2002. Accessed January 29, 2020. https://www.childtrends.org.
Hammond, Zaretta. *Culturally Responsive Teaching & the Brain: Promoting Authentic Engagement and Rigor among Culturally and Linguistically Diverse Students.* Thousand Oaks, California: Corwin, 2015.
Hanna, Maddie and Kristen A. Graham. "Which Are the Best, Most Improved Philly Schools? District Reveals Them." *Philadelphia Inquirer*, February 10, 2020. https://www.inquirer.com.
Harris Jr., Rafael S. "Racial Microaggression? How Do You Know?" *American Psychologist* 63, no. 4 (2008): 275–276.
Hart, Betty and Todd R. Risley. *Meaningful Differences in the Everyday Experience of Young American Children.* Baltimore, MD: Paul R. Brookes Publishing Co., 1995.
Hartmann, Douglas, Joseph Gerteis, and Paul R. Croll. "An Empirical Assessment of Whiteness Theory: Hidden from How Many?" *Society for the Study of Social Problems* 56, no. 3 (August 2009): 403–424.
Hawkins, David R. *Power vs. Force: The Hidden Determinants of Human Behavior.* West Sedona, AZ: Veritas Publishing, 2013.
Hendrickson, Beccah. "Heartwarming: Teacher Adopts Student from Philadelphia School." 6ABC Action News, December 19, 2019. Accessed February 12, 2020. https://www.6abc.com.
Higgins, Charlotte. "The Age of Patriarchy: How an Unfashionable Idea Became a Rallying Cry for Feminism Today." *The Guardian*, June 22, 2018. https://www.theguardian.com.
Hsieh, Evelyn. "Following Obama, Students Define 'Black' on Ivy League Campuses," *Huff Post*, June 19, 2009. https://www.huffpost.com.
Hughes, Coleman. "The Racism Treadmill." *Quillette*, May 14, 2018. https://quillette.com.
Jussim, Lee. "Mandatory Implicit Bias Training Is a Bad Idea." *Psychology Today*, December 2, 2017. https://www.psychologytoday.com.
Kendi, Ibram X. *How to Be an Antiracist.* New York: One World, 2019.
Kirsanow, Peter. "Racial Disparities and School Discipline." *National Review*, July 25, 2019. https://www.nationalreview.com.
Kupers, Terry A. "Toxic Masculinity as a Barrier to Mental Health Treatment in Prison." *Journal of Clinical Psychology* 61, no. 6 (2005): 714.
Lam, Charles. "Harvard Announces High Admittance of Asian Americans as Judge Weighs Affirmative Action." NBC News, April 2, 2019. Accessed January 22, 2020. https://www.nbcnews.com.
Lawrence, Sandra M. and Beverly Daniel Tatum. "White Racial Identity and Anti-Racist Education: A Catalyst for Change." Teaching for Change. Accessed December 31, 2019. https://www.teachingforchange.org.
Lilienfeld, Scott O. "Microaggressions: Strong Claims, Inadequate Evidence." *Perspectives on Psychological Science* 12, no. 1 (2017): 138–169.
Ludwig, Jack. "Acceptance of Interracial Marriage at Record High." *Gallup*, June 1, 2004. https://www.gallup.com.

Lynch, Megan E. "The Hidden Nature of Whiteness in Education: Creating Active Allies in White Teachers." *Journal of Educational Supervision* 1, no. 1 (2018): 18–31.
Mac Donald, Heather. "Police Shootings and Race." *Washington Post*, July 18, 2016. https://www.washingtonpost.com.
Maharaj, Ranjit. *Illusion vs. Reality*. Sadguru Publishing, 2010.
Markowicz, Karol. "Quit the Racial Demagoguery and Start Working for Better Schools." *New York Post*, November 24, 2019. https://nypost.com.
McIntosh, Peggy. "White Privilege: Unpacking the Invisible Knapsack." *Peace and Freedom Magazine*, July/August, 1989.
Mezzacappa, Dale. "District Settles with Feds on South Philly HS." *Philadelphia Public School Notebook*, December 15, 2010. https://thenotebook.org.
Michael, Ali. *Raising Race Questions: Whiteness, Inquiry and Education*. New York: Teachers College Press, 2015.
Mills, Charles. *The Racial Contract*. New York: Cornell University Press, 1997.
Ming Liu, William, Rossina Zamora Liu, Younkyoung Loh Garrison, Ji Youn Cindy Kim, Laurence Chan, Yu C. S. Ho, and Chi W. Yeung. "Racial Trauma, Microaggressions, and Becoming Racially Innocuous: The Role of Acculturation and White Supremacist Ideology." *American Psychologist* 74, no. 1 (2019): 143–155.
National Education Association, New Business Item 4 (2018), 2018. Accessed January 25, 2020. https://ra.nea.org.
National Fatherhood Initiative. "Father Facts 8," 2019. Accessed January 26, 2020. https://www.fatherhood.org.
NBC News. "Democratic Debate Transcript: July 31, 2019." Accessed January 18, 2020. https://www.nbcnews.com.
NBC10 Philadelphia. "Listen: Manager's 911 Call Before Arrest of 2 Black Men at Philly Starbucks." April 17, 2018. Accessed December 31, 2019. https://www.nbcphiladelphia.com.
NBC10 Philadelphia. "'There Will Be No Teachers Left': Educators in Philadelphia Talk about Quitting, School Violence and Paying for Classroom Supplies." February 4, 2020. Accessed February 11, 2020. https://www.nbcphiladelphia.com.
Newport, Frank. "Fewer Blacks in U.S. See Bias in Jobs, Income, and Housing." *Gallup*, July 19, 2013. https://news.gallup.com.
Newton Moses, Sheila. "Understanding the Academic Success of Black Caribbean Immigrant Students Who Have Earned a Graduate Degree at an Ivy League University." Doctoral Dissertation, Seton Hall University, College of Education and Human Services, May 18, 2019. https://scholarship.shu.edu.
Niemonen, Jack. "Antiracist Education in Theory and Practice: A Critical Assessment." *The American Sociologist* 38, no. 2 (June 2007): 159–177.
NPR, WSIU Radio. "Brittney Cooper: How Has Time Been Stolen from People of Color?" March 29, 2019. https://news.wsiu.org.
Pappas, Stephanie. "APA Issues First-Ever Guidelines for Practice with Men and Boys." *American Psychological Association* 50, no. 1 (2019): 34.
Parratt, John. "Time in Traditional African Thought." *Religion* 7, no. 2 (1977): 117–126.
Paslay, Christopher. "Ancient Chinese Secret: Why Asian Students Excel Academically." *Chalk and Talk*, December 16, 2012. https://chalkandtalk.wordpress.com.
Paslay, Christopher. "Commentary: Skip Black Lives Matter's Action Week in Philly schools." *Philadelphia Inquirer*, January 19, 2017. https://www.inquirer.com.
Paslay, Christopher. "Diversity Training Shouldn't Be Based on Flawed Implicit Bias Research." *Philadelphia Inquirer*, June 14, 2019. https://www.inquirer.com.
Pennsylvania Keystone Exams. 2019 English Keystone Summary Report, Swenson Arts and Technology HS, Philadelphia City SD, Spring 2019.
Pew Research Center. "On Views of Race and Inequality, Blacks and Whites Are Worlds Apart." June 27, 2016. https://www.pewsocialtrends.org.
Philadelphia Futures. "Success Stories." Accessed February 2, 2020. https://philadelphiafutures.org.

Ponterotto, Joseph G., Shawn O. Utsey and Paul B. Pedersen. *Preventing Prejudice: A Guide for Counselors, Educators, and Parents*. Thousand Oaks, California: Sage Publications, 2006.
Project Implicit. "Preliminary Information." Accessed January 11, 2020. https://implicit.harvard.edu/implicit/takeatest.html.
Rosenthal, Robert and Lenore Jacobson. *Pygmalion in the Classroom: Teacher Expectation and Pupils' Intellectual Development*. New York: Holt, Rinehart and Winston, 1968.
Salter, Michael. "The Problem with a Fight against Toxic Masculinity." *The Atlantic*, February 27, 2019. https://www.theatlantic.com.
Sanneh, Kelefa. "The Fight to Redefine Racism." *The New Yorker*, August 12, 2019. https://www.newyorker.com.
Schacht, Thomas E. "A Broader View of Racial Microaggression in Psychotherapy." *American Psychologist* 63, no. 4 (2008): 273.
Singal, Jesse. "Psychology's Favorite Tool for Measuring Racism Isn't Up to the Job." *The Cut*, January 11, 2017. https://www.thecut.com.
Singal, Jesse. "The Creators of the Implicit Association Test Should Get Their Story Straight." *Intelligencer*, December 5, 2017. http://nymag.com/intelligencer.
Smith, Mychal Denzel. "The Dangerous Myth of the 'Missing Black Father'." *Washington Post*, January 10, 2017. https://www.washingtonpost.com.
Snyder, Susan, John Sullivan, Kristen A. Graham and Dylan Purcell. "Children Ages 5 to 10 Assault Staff and Classmates. Some Commit Sex Offenses." *Philadelphia Inquirer*, March 29, 2011. https://www.inquirer.com.
Snyder, Susan, Kristen A. Graham, John Sullivan, and Dylan Purcell. "Violence Targets Teachers, Staff." *Philadelphia Inquirer*, March 30, 2011. https://www.inquirer.com.
Spencer, Kyle. "For Asians, School Tests Are Vital Steppingstones." *New York Times*, October 26, 2012. https://www.nytimes.com.
Spencer, Steven J., Christine Logel, and Paul G. Davies. "Stereotype Threat." *Annual Review of Psychology* 67, (2016): 415–437.
Stroessner, Steve and Catherine Good. "Stereotype Threat: An Overview." Reducing Stereotype Threat. Accessed December 3, 2020. http://www.reducingstereotypethreat.org.
Sullivan, John, Susan Snyder, Kristen A. Graham, and Dylan Purcell. "Climate of Violence Stifles City Schools." *Philadelphia Inquirer*, March 27, 2011. https://www.inquirer.com.
Sy, Aminata. "Philadelphia's Many African Students Need Culturally Inclusive Education." *Philadelphia Inquirer*, February 19, 2019. https://www.inquirer.com.
Takaki, Ronald. *A Different Mirror: A History of Multicultural America*. New York: Back Bay Books, 1993.
Taylor, Kate. "Sephora Will Temporarily Close All Its Stores on Wednesday." *Business Insider*, June 4, 2019. https://www.businessinsider.com.
Teach for America Greater Philadelphia, Certification & Training. Accessed January 26, 2020. https://www.teachforamerica.org.
The Conscious Kid. "Critical Conversations: Dr. Robin DiAngelo on White Fragility and Why It's So Hard for White People to Talk about Racism." Accessed November 30, 2019. https://www.theconsciouskid.org.
The New Teacher Project. "The Opportunity Myth," 2018. Accessed February 21, 2020. https://opportunitymyth.tntp.org.
The Pulitzer Prizes. "The 2012 Pulitzer Prize Winner in Public Service." Accessed February 4, 2020. https://www.pulitzer.org.
The School District of Philadelphia. "9/27 Equity vs. Equality." Office of Teaching and Learning, Student Rights and Responsibilities, September 27, 2019.
The School District of Philadelphia. "PD Survey: September 27, 2019." Office of Research and Evaluation, October 2019.
The School District of Philadelphia. "Teachers of the Month for October and November." November 26, 2019. Accessed February 12, 2020. https://www.philasd.org.
Thomas, Kenneth R. "Macrononsense in Multiculturalism." *American Psychologist* 63, no. 4 (2008): 274–275.

Tornoe, Rob. "What Happened at Starbucks in Philadelphia?" *Philadelphia Inquirer*, April 16, 2018. https://www.inquirer.com.

Truss, Joe. "What Happened When My School Started to Dismantle White Supremacy Culture." *Education Week*, July 18, 2019. https://www.edweek.org.

U.S. Commission on Civil Rights. *Beyond Suspensions: Examining School Discipline Policies and Connections to the School-to-Prison Pipeline for Students of Color with Disabilities.* Washington, DC, July 2019. https://www.usccr.gov/pubs/2019/07-23-Beyond-Suspensions.pdf.

U.S. Department of Education, Office for Civil Rights. "Joint 'Dear Colleague' Letter." January 8, 2014. Accessed February 14, 2020. https://www2ed.gov.

U.S. News & World Report. "Best Pennsylvania High Schools," 2019. Accessed February 2, 2020. https://www.usnews.com.

Van Der Valk, Adrienne and Anya Malley. "What's My Complicity? Talking White Fragility With Robin DiAngelo." *Teaching Tolerance* 62, (Summer 2019). https://www.tolerance.org.

Wing Sue, Derald, Christina M. Capodilupo, Gina C. Torino, Jennifer M. Bucceri, Aisha M. B. Holder, Kevin L. Nadal, and Marta Esquilin. "Racial Microaggressions in Everyday Life." *American Psychologist* 62, no. 4 (2007): 271–286.

Wing Sue, Derald, Sarah Alsaidi, Michael N. Awad, Elizabeth Glaeser, Cassandra Z. Calle, and Narolyn Mendez. "Disarming Racial Microaggressions: Microintervention Strategies for Targets, White Allies, and Bystanders." *American Psychologist* 74, no. 1 (2019): 128–142.

Index

Ababio-Fernandez, Ruby, 43, 44
abuse, 63
academic performance, stereotype threat and, xvi–xvii
Ackerman, Arlene C., 50, 78
Adamson-White, Debontina, 79
ADVIS. *See* Association of Delaware Valley Independent Schools
affirmative action, 122
African Americans, 17–18, 64, 66, 67, 87
Africans, 48, 51–53, 57
Alexander, Michelle, 89
American Dream, 105–110
American Mosaic Project, 12–13
American Psychological Association (APA), 67
anti-bias trainings, 17, 18; with diversity conference, 35–40; mandatory vs. voluntary, 40–41, 45; recommendations, 45; in schools, xvi
anti-bias workshops, xi, 26–27
anti-blackness, 36–37, 121
antiracism, xvi, 15, 18, 38; education and, 4–6, 26; with "Equity vs. Equality" training, 30–32; multiculturalism vs., 4–6
anti-whiteness, 36–37, 38
APA. *See* American Psychological Association
"The ARC of the United States", 11
Arnesen, Eric, 2, 23

Aronson, Joshua, 102–103
Aryan Nation, 10
Asian Americans, 42, 48, 49–51
Asian Americans United, 50
Association of Delaware Valley Independent Schools (ADVIS), 4, 35
Augustana College, 2
Austin, Lou, 77–78

Banaji, Mahzarin, 16, 41
Banks, James A., 113–114, 115
Barron, Carrie, 102
behavior, 63, 80, 90–91, 95
"Beyond Suspensions" (U.S. Commission on Civil Rights), 85
birth, race and conditions of, ix–x
"blackface" controversy, 10
Black Lives Matter, 56–57
Buddhism, 116, 117–118

cancer, racism and, 6
Carranza, Richard, xvi, 11, 41, 42, 43, 44
Carson, Ben, 109
Castagno, Angela E., 5
Caucus of Working Educators, 56–57
Census Bureau, U.S., 51
"Challenging toxic masculinity in schools and society" (Elliott), 68
"Charting Parenthood" (Child Trends), 65
"check your privilege", 7, 8

children, 62, 63, 64, 65–66; ECLS, 50, 86; parents, race and, 62–63, 64, 66; violence and, 75–78
Child Trends, 65
Chinese Exclusion Act (1882), 49
Chislett, Leslie, 43–44
Chomsky, Noam, 80
Church, Jonathan: with white fragility theory, criticism of, xvi, 9, 32–33; on whiteness studies, criticism of, 24; on white privilege, 8
civil rights, 5, 12, 85, 88, 92
Cody, Jackie, 42
Collins, Cory, 7
colorblindness, 2, 53, 54; individualism and, 12–15; recommendations, 19, 81
colorism, 51, 53
Commission on Civil Rights, U.S., 85, 88
Confucianism, 51
Cooper, Brittney, 57
coping mechanism, learning with violence as, 73–75
Crenshaw, Kimberlé, 68
crime, 63, 73, 75–78
Critical Race Theory (CRT), 5, 54, 55
Croll, Paul R., 2, 12–13, 23
CRT. *See* Critical Race Theory
Crusius, Patrick, 10
cultural deficit theory, 8
Cultural Diversity and Education (Banks), 113, 114, 115
Culturally Responsive Teaching & the Brain (Hammond), 75, 107
culture, xvi, 3–4, 47, 48; Asian Americans and, 49–51; multicultural ideology, 113–115, 123; multiculturalism and, 4–6, 29, 38, 123; recommendations, 58; with universal values, racialization of, 54–58; West Indian and African immigrants, 51–53

danger discourse, 71–73, 74
"The Dangerous Myth of the 'Missing Black Father'" (Smith, M. D.), 64
Davies, Paul G., 103, 104
"Dear Colleague" letter, 85, 89–90, 91, 95
"Dear White Teacher", 119
deaths, 63, 64
de Blasio, Bill, 42
Department of Education, U.S., xvii, 89, 90
Department of Justice, U.S., 50, 89
DeVos, Betsy, 92
DiAngelo, Robin, ix, x–xi, xv, 2, 4, 15, 121; on colorblindness, 12, 13, 53; criticism of, xvi, 9, 12–13, 24, 32–33, 39–40, 48, 117, 120; as diversity conference leader, 35–40; implicit bias and, 25; on individualism, 14; on people of color and racism, 3–4; on racism, redefining, 10; on whiteness, 100–101; with white supremacy redefined, 10–11. *See also* white fragility theory
A Different Mirror (Takaki), 49
"Disarming Racial Microaggressions" (Sue et al.), 29
discipline, xvii, 92–94. *See also* racial disparities, school discipline and
"Discipline Reform through the Eyes of Teachers" (Fordham Institute), xvii, 92–94
Dismantling Racism (Jones and Okun), 41
disparity fallacy, 47, 48
"Disrupting Your Texts" (Ebarvia), 56, 108
#Disrupttexts, 56, 107–108, 109
diversity, through unity: with heart not mind, 117–120; magic of, 120–123; multicultural ideology and, 113–115, 123; with racism redefined, 116; recommendations, 123
diversity conference, 35–40
Doane, Ashley, 23
Downie, Blair, 79
Du Bois, W. E. B., 1
Dyson, Michael Eric, 38

Early Childhood Longitudinal Study (ECLS), 50, 86
Early Life Stress Research Program, 102
Ebarvia, Tricia, 56, 108
Ebonics, 56
ECLS. *See* Early Childhood Longitudinal Study
economy, 47, 50, 53, 62, 64, 65
education, xvi–xvii, 56, 58, 89, 90, 99, 123; African American women and, 47; Africans and, 52–53; antiracist, 4–6, 26;

Asian Americans and, 49–51; Department Of Education lawsuit, New York, 43; diversity conference and, 35–40; parents and attainment of, 67–69; problem-posing, 55; reform, 61–62; Seattle school district, 55–56; STPP and, 87–89; television and, 66; whiteness studies and, 97; "White Racial Identity and Anti-Racist Education", 2–3; white supremacy and, 25; with white supremacy redefined, 11. *See also* teachers

Educational Testing Service (ETS), 61, 65, 66, 99
educators, 18, 56–57, 58. *See also* teachers
Eliot, T. S., 14
Elliott, Kathleen, 68
El Paso Massacre (2019), 10
"An Empirical Assessment of Whiteness Theory" (Hartmann, Gerteis and Croll), 2, 12–13, 23
"The Epistemological Problem of White Fragility Theory" (Church), 32–33
"Equity vs. Equality" training, 30–32
Ertel, Mike, 10
ETS. *See* Educational Testing Service
European Association of Social Psychology study, 103
expectations, power of, 97–102; American Dream and, 105–110; recommendations, 110; stereotype threat and, 102–104
"The Family—America's Smallest School" (ETS), 65

Father Facts, Eighth Edition (NFI), 62, 69
fathers, 62–65, 69
Federal Interagency Forum on Child and Family Statistics, 65–66
Fennessy, Sean, 78
Fordham Institute, xvii, 92–94
Freire, Paulo, 54–55

Gallup poll (2013), 53
Garcia, Melissa, 27–28
Garrison, William Lloyd, 7
Gates, Henry Lewis, 67
gender, race and, 68
Gerteis, Joseph, 2, 12–13, 23

Gillibrand, Kirsten, 8
Gonzales, Matt, 42
Goodwin, Michael, 42
Graham, Kristin, 76
Graves Williamson, Toni, 36, 37, 38
Greenwald, Anthony, 16, 41
"Guidelines for Psychological Practice With Boys and Men" (APA), 67
Gym, Helen, 50

Hammond, Zaretta, 75, 107
Hardin-Bey, John, 81
Harris, Rafael, S., Jr., 29
Hart, Betty, 66
Hartmann, Douglas, 2, 12–13, 23
Hawkins, David R., 121
Helms, Janet E., 3
Heriot, Gail, 85, 86–88, 90, 91
Herring, Teshada, 76–77
"The Hidden Nature of Whiteness in Education" (Lynch), 97–98
Higgins, Charlotte, 68
Hlat, Penny, 79
Holder, Eric, xv
Holocaust, xvi, 42
hostile, whiteness as, 36, 38
hostile environments, whites in, xvi, 43
Hughes, Coleman, 47–48

IAT. *See* Implicit Association Test
"I Have a Dream" speech (King), 12
immigrants, 48, 51–53. *See also* Asian Americans
impact, intent vs., 15–18
Implicit Association Test (IAT), 16, 25–26, 27
implicit bias, 16, 41; overuse of, 24–28, 40–41; Starbucks incident and, 17
individualism, 2; colorblindness and, 12–15; skewed concept of, 14
infant mortality, 64
intent: impact vs., 15–18; recommendations, 19; Starbucks incident and, 17–18
internalized oppression, 100, 103, 107
International Literacy Association, 56
interracial marriage, 24
intersectionality, 68
Iqbal, Riyan, 50–51

Ivy League schools, 50, 52

Jacobson, Lenore, 100
Johnson, Kevin, 17
Jones, Kenneth, 41
Jussim, Lee, 40–41, 103
Justice Department, U.S., xvii

Kendi, Ibram X., 47
Keystone Exam scores, 106–107
King, Martin Luther, Jr., 5, 12
Kirsanow, Peter, 85, 86, 87, 91
Ku Klux Klan, 10
Kupers, Terry, 68

Lawrence, Sandra M., 2–3
learning: danger discourse and, 71–73; recommendations, 81–82; with teachers dedicated to positive change, 78–81, 82; with transparency, courage of, 75–78; with violence as coping mechanism, 73–75
The Liberator (newspaper), 7
Lilienfeld, Scott O., 16
literacy, children and, 65–66
Liu, Lucas, 43
Logel, Christine, 103, 104
Lynch, Megan E., 97–98

Maharaj, Ranjit, 116
Malvern Preparatory School, 35–40
Markowicz, Karol, 42–43
marriage, 51, 52
masculinity, toxic, 67–69
Mastermann, Julia R., 80
math, ethnocentric, 55–56
Matsui, Robert, 49
McCloskey, Kelly, 79
McCloskey, Santo, 79
McDermott, Monica, 23
McIntosh, Peggy, 1, 7, 100
Meaningful Differences in the Everyday Experience of Young American Children (Hart and Risley), 66
men, 63, 67; as fathers, 62–65; oppression of black, 64
Merriam-Webster, 9, 10, 15
methodology: epistemological problems, 32–33; implicit bias, overuse of, 24–28;
microaggressions, 28–32; recommendations, 33; whiteness studies without scientific rigor, 23–24
Michael, Ali, 36, 37–38
microaggression research program (MRP), 16
microaggressions, 16; dubious nature of, 28–32, 33; workshop recommendations, 33
"Microaggressions" (Lilienfeld), 16
microassaults, 28
microinsults, 28
microinvalidations, 28–29
Mills, Charles M., 11
mind, with overthinking race, 117–120
model minorities, systemic racism and, 49
monologue, race as, xi, xv
Moses, Sheila Newton, 52–53
mothers, economy and single, 65
Moynihan, Daniel Patrick, 66, 67
The Moynihan Report Revisited, 67
MRP. *See* microaggression research program
multicultural ideology, 113–115, 123
multiculturalism, 29, 123; antiracism vs., 4–6; universal values and, 38. *See also* culture

National Fatherhood Initiative (NFI), 62, 63, 69
National Longitudinal Study of Adolescent Health, 63
National Survey on Drug Use and Health (2012), 63
"The Negro Family" (Moynihan), 66, 67
new racism, 24–25, 54
New York: with discipline, 93–94; with DOE lawsuit, 43–44; with racial environment, toxic, 41–44; shootings and race in, 72
New York Post (newspaper), 41–43, 44
New York Times (newspaper), 50, 51
NFI. *See* National Fatherhood Initiative
niceness, antiracism and, 4–5
Niemonen, Jack, 4, 5–6
Nosek, Brian, 16, 41
now, power of, 120, 123
Núñez, Priscilla, 81

Obama, Barack, 24, 85, 122
Office of Student Rights and Responsibilities, 26–27
Of Mice and Men (Steinbeck), 105, 109, 110
Okun, Tema, 41
oppression, 64, 100, 103, 107, 115
Othello (Shakespeare), 109–110

parents: "Charting Parenthood", 65; with children and literacy, 65–66; economy and single mothers, 65; educational attainment of, 67–69; father facts, 62–65; race of children living with, 62–63, 64, 66. *See also* patriarchy, parents and
Parks, Tyree, 77
"Parsing the Achievement Gap II" (ETS), 66
patriarchy, parents and: education reform and, 61–62; etymology, 68; father facts, 62–65; with masculinity, toxic, 67–69; recommendations, 69
PBIS. *See* Positive Behavior Interventions and Supports
Pedagogy of the Oppressed (Freire), 54–55
Pennsylvania Value-Added Assessment System (PVAAS), 107, 110
people of color, racism and, 3–4
Perry, Davida, 43
Pew Research Center, 51
Pew Research studies, 12–13, 52, 53
Philadelphia Inquirer (newspaper), 51–52, 75–78
Philadelphia School District: Africans in, 52; crime and violence in, 75–78; "Equity vs. Equality" training, 30–32; Keystone Exam scores, 106–107; Office of Student Rights and Responsibilities, 26–27; with racial discrimination and violence, 49–50; SPR, 80; teachers with positive change in, 78–81; with teacher turnover, 61
Pierce, Chester M., 28
PISA. *See* Programme for International Student Assessment
Pitts, Melvin, 81
Plato's cave, 24
police, 7, 17–18

political activism, whiteness studies and, 2
politics, 3–4, 8
Positive Behavior Interventions and Supports (PBIS), 80
post-traumatic stress disorder (PTSD), 75, 102
poverty, 62, 67, 81–82, 93
power: of accumulated power, 7; of now, 120, 123; white fragility theory and true, 121; white privilege and manifestations of, 7; white supremacist culture with political, 3–4. *See also* expectations, power of
"Power vs. Force" (Hawkins), 121
prajna wisdom, 117–118
The Price of Nice (Castagno), 5
Princeton University, 52
prisons, 87–89
privilege, white supremacists and, 3, 6, 15. *See also* white privilege
problem-posing education, 55
Programme for International Student Assessment (PISA), 56, 58, 99
PTSD. *See* post-traumatic stress disorder
Purcell, Dylan, 76
PVAAS. *See* Pennsylvania Value-Added Assessment System
Pygmalion Effect, 100
Pygmalion in the Classroom (Rosenthal and Jacobson), 100

race, 37; American Dream and, 105; birth conditions shaped by, ix–x; of children living with parents, 62–63, 64, 66; crime and, 73; CRT, 5, 54, 55; economy and, 47, 50, 53; gender and, 68; linear time and, 57–58; as monologue, xi, xv; overthinking, 117–120; racism and, 14; shootings and, 72; standardized tests and, xvi, 50; stereotype threat and, xvi; violence and, 87; white privilege and, xi
racial discrimination, violence and, 49–50
racial disparities, school discipline and: in context, 85–87; race-based discipline and, 89–92; recommendations, 94–95; STPP and, 87–89
"Racial Disparities and School Discipline" (Kirsanow), 91

racial environment, New York with toxic, 41–44
racial identity, WRID theory and, 2–3
racial inequality, 31, 47, 48, 53, 58
racialization, 54–58
"Racial Microaggression? How Do You Know?" (Harris), 29
"Racial Microaggressions in Everyday Life" (Sue et al.), 28
racial profiling, at Sephora, 18
racial status quo, as racism, xv
The Racial Contract (Mills), 11
racism, 41; accusations of, 10; cancer and, 6; colorblind, 12; colorblindness and, 53, 54; defined, 9; new, 24–25, 54; people of color and, 3–4; perpetuation of, xi, 2; race and, 14; racial status quo as, xv; redefined, 1–2, 10, 11, 18, 116; scientific method and, 6; scientific method as epistemology of, 55; white fragility theory and, ix, 9; and whiteness, 2; white supremacy and, 9–12. *See also* antiracism; systemic racism
Raising Race Questions (Michael), 37
reform, education, 61–62
Reilly, Donald F., 35
Renee, Deonca, 44
reparations, for slavery, 47
Risley, Todd R., 66
Rosenthal, Robert, 100
Ross, Richard, 17

Sa-kiera T. J. Hudson, 103
Samson, Frank, 23
Schacht, Thomas, E., 29–30
school discipline, 92–94. *See also* racial disparities, school discipline and
School Performance Report (SPR), 80
schools: anti-bias trainings in, xvi; discipline guidelines in, xvii
School-to-Prison Pipeline (STPP), 87–89
science: behind IAT, 16, 25–26, 27; behind implicit bias, 16; behind microaggressions, 16; whiteness studies with rigor of, 23–24
scientific method: with objective universal rational inquiry, 33; racism and, 6; as racist epistemology, 55

Seattle school district, 55–56
self-affirmation, 104
Sephora, racial profiling at, 18
Shakespeare, William, 109–110
Sherman, 104
Shi, Ting, 50, 51
shootings, 72, 77
Singal, Jesse, 25–26
slavery, 47, 106, 115, 122
Smith, Mychal Denzel, 64
Smollett, Jussie, 10
Snyder, Sue, 76
Society of Professors of Education Outstanding Book Award (2017), 37
Sowell, Thomas, 47
Spencer, Steven, J., 103, 104
SPR. *See* School Performance Report
standardized tests, race and, xvi, 50
Stanford University, 102
Starbucks incident, 17–18
Steele, Claude, 102–103, 104
Steinbeck, John, 105, 109, 110
stereotype threat, xvi, 40; academic performance influenced by, xvi–xvii; with expectations, power of, 102–104
STPP. *See* School-to-Prison Pipeline
Students for Fair Admissions, 50
substance abuse, men and, 63
Sue, Derald Wing, 28, 29
Sullivan, John, 76
Sy, Aminata, 51–52
systemic oppression, of Asian Americans, 49
systemic racism, 1, 49, 87; perpetuation of, 25, 121–122; racial inequality and, 31, 47, 53, 58; as too ingrained for improvement, 36
SZA, 18

Takaki, Ronald, 49
Tatum, Beverly Daniel, 2–3
teachers: with anti-bias training, xvi; "Dear White Teacher", 119; "Discipline Reform Through the Eyes of Teachers", xvii; educators, 18, 56–57, 58; with "Equity vs. Equality" training, 30–32; positive change and dedicated, 78–81, 82; school discipline and, 92–94; TNTP, 101–102; turnover, 61; violence

against, 77–78
Teach for America, 62
Teaching Tolerance (DiAngelo), 15
television, education and, 66

The New Teacher Project (TNTP), 101–102

Thomas, Kenneth R., 29
time, race and linear, 57–58
TNTP. *See* The New Teacher Project
Tolle, Eckhart, 120
toxicity: with masculinity and patriarchy, 67–69; of racial environment, New York, 41–44
trainings: implicit bias, 41; mandatory vs. voluntary anti-bias, 40–41, 45. *See also* anti-bias trainings
transparency, courage of, 75–78
true power, white fragility theory and, 121
"Understanding the Academic Success of Black Caribbean Immigrant Students Who Have Earned a Graduate Degree at an Ivy League University" (Moses), 52–53

United States (U.S.): Census Bureau, 51; Commission on Civil Rights, 85, 88, 92; Department of Education, xvii, 89, 90; Department of Justice, 50, 89; with global education gap, 56; Justice Department, xvii
unity, magic of, 120–123. *See also* diversity, through unity
universal values, 116, 119; multiculturalism and, 38; racialization of, 54–58
University of California study, 52
University of Iowa, 54
University of Maryland, 54
University of Minnesota, 2
University of Pennsylvania, 52
U.S. News & World Report, 56, 80

values, racialization of universal, 54–58
violence: child abuse, 63; as coping mechanism with learning, 73–75; race and, 87; racial discrimination and, 49–50; recommendations, 81; shootings, 72, 77; against teachers, 77–78; transparency and, 75–78

Washington Post (newspaper), 64
West, Cornel, 67
West Indian immigrants, 51–53
What Does It Mean To Be White? (DiAngelo), ix, 3–4, 100; colorblind racism and, 12; danger discourse in, 71–73; diversity conference with, 36; with racism redefined, 10; with white supremacy redefined, 10–11
"What Happened When My School Started to Dismantle White Supremacy Culture" (blog), 11
white fragility: accusations of, 8–9; defined, xv; with questions unanswered, 37; white privilege and, 6–9
White Fragility (DiAngelo), 120; diversity conference with, 35–40; racial stress and, 9
white fragility theory: creation of, 41; criticism of, xvi, 9, 24, 32–33; implementation of, 44; racism and, ix, 9; true power and, 121; views on, 39–40, 43
whiteness: defined, 38, 100–101; as hostile, 36, 38; racism and, 2
"Whiteness and the Historians' Imagination" (Arnesen), 23
whiteness studies: colorblindness and, 12; education and, 97; empirical study on, 45; recommendations, 18; without scientific rigor, 23–24
whiteness studies, tenets: aim of, 2; colorblindness and individualism with, 12–15; defined, 1, 2; with impact vs. intent, 15–18; mission of, 1; multiculturalism vs. antiracism, 4–6; political activism and, 2; with racism and white supremacy, 9–12; recommendations, 18–19; utility of, 2; with whiteness redefined, 1–2; white privilege and white fragility, 6–9; WRID theory and, 2–3
"Whiteness Studies" (Church), 24
white privilege: "check your", 7, 8; connotations, 7; eliminating, 7–8; with

manifestations of power, 7; police and, 7; politics and, 8; race and, xi; white fragility and, 6–9; whiteness studies and, 2
"White Privilege" (McIntosh), 1, 7, 100
"White Privilege Exercise", 41–42
"White Racial Identity and Anti-Racist Education" (Lawrence and Tatum), 2–3
white racial identity development (WRID) theory, 2–3, 98, 118
white racial literacy, ix, xv, xvi, 3, 12
whites, in hostile environments, xvi, 43
white silence, xv, 39
white supremacists: culture with political power, 3–4; defined, 10; ideology, 54; privilege and, 3, 6, 15; society, 37, 105
white supremacy: accusations of, 10, 37; antiracism and, 6; Asian Americans and, 42, 48; cultural deficit theory and, 8; culture, xvi; defined, 10; education and, 25; maintaining, xv; perpetuation of, 2; progressive version of, 11; racism and, 9–12; redefined, 10–11
The White-Black Achievement Gap (ETS), 99
Why Are All the Black Kids Sitting Together in the Cafeteria? (Tatum), 3
"Why Teachers Must Fight Their Own Implicit Biases" (Garcia), 27–28
Williams, Terrance, 81
Wilson, William Julius, 67
women: economy and single mothers, 65; education and African American, 47
WRID theory. *See* white racial identity development theory

X, Malcolm, 5

Zen Buddhism, 117–118

About the Author

Christopher Paslay is a longtime Philadelphia public schoolteacher, education writer, and track coach. He's a certified Pennsylvania school counselor with an MEd in Multicultural Education. His articles on school reform have appeared in numerous publications, including *The Philadelphia Inquirer*, *The Federalist*, and *Real Clear Politics*.

www.ingramcontent.com/pod-product-compliance
Lightning Source LLC
Chambersburg PA
CBHW030141240426
43672CB00005B/219